FROZEN YOGURT

by Mable & Gar Hoffman

FISHER
BOOKS

**Library of Congress
Cataloging-in-Publication Data**
Hoffman, Mable, 1922-
  [Frozen yogurt]
  Mable Hoffman's frozen yogurt / by Mable
    and Gar Hoffman
      p. c.m
  ISBN 1-55561-035-8
  1. Frozen yogurt. I. Hoffman, Gar. II. Title.
TX795.H689   1990
641.8'62—dc20   90-33173
                                              CIP

Publishers: Bill Fisher
                Helen Fisher
                Howard Fisher
                Tom Monroe, P.E.

Editors: Bill Fisher
                Joyce Bush

Book Production: Karen McGraw

Art Director: Josh Young

Drawings: David Fischer

Research Assistant: Jan Robertson

Cover photo: DeGennaro Associates

Published by Fisher Books
PO Box 38040
Tucson, AZ 85740-8040
(602) 292-9080

© 1990 Fisher Books

Printed in U.S.A.
Printing 10 9 8 7 6 5 4 3 2

Notice: The information in this book is true
and complete to the best of our knowledge.
It is offered with no guarantees on the part of
the authors or Fisher Books. Authors and
publisher disclaim all liability in connection
with the use of this book.

Table of Contents

A Culinary Love Story

The past decade has seen an unimaginable growth of frozen-yogurt shops. Few, if any, new food creations have been so enthusiastically embraced by the public as has frozen yogurt. The "magnets" that have drawn us to frozen-yogurt shops are the popularity of yogurt itself and the convenience the shops afford us in acquiring ready-made frozen yogurt. Plus, there's the fulfillment of our unrelenting quest for more healthful foods, especially beneficial desserts.

As for convenience, frozen-yogurt shops offer the consumer two advantages. You expend no effort in producing the product and it is not necessary to wait out the preparation and freezing processes; it is ready-made for immediate enjoyment at the shops. Homemade frozen yogurt offers significant advantages over its commercial counterpart. First off, commercial shops offer a very limited number of flavors. Flavor considerations are almost unlimited when you make your own. Then, too, you don't have to leave home to enjoy this delightful dessert. But most important, homemade frozen yogurt affords the opportunity to produce a dish that is more attuned to your taste and dietary life style. For instance, you have total control of the ingredients used. You can vary its tanginess and sweetness. And you can adjust fat, caloric and cholesterol content. Perhaps the greatest plus in making your own frozen yogurt is the opportunity to savor those wonderful fresh-fruit flavors, instead of tolerating a product made of those same-tasting fruit-flavored syrups commonly used by frozen-yogurt shops.

Making frozen yogurt *your way* instills great satisfaction in knowing the ingredients are compatible with your dietary life style. Here's to your health and raptured enjoyment!

The How & Why of Frozen Yogurt

A few minutes devoted to reading this chapter will greatly enhance the pleasures of creating and enjoying frozen yogurts, the likes of which commercial shops can only dream about.

About Quality

In making your own frozen yogurt, you control the freshness and quality of the ingredients used. And you can select from a wide range of fresh, natural flavors. You can completely eliminate preservatives, chemical emulsifiers and artificial flavors.

About Quantity

Each recipe in this book makes about 1 quart, that is, 3 to 4 cups. However, the ingredients can easily be doubled or quadrupled should you want to make half a gallon or one gallon, respectively. We are not being wishy-washy when we use the phrase, "Makes *about* 1 quart." We use the word *about* because many factors affect the quantity that each recipe yields. The ingredients used, the freezing method selected and the temperature of the prepared ingredients prior to freezing all relate to the quantity of the frozen product. In general, ingredients such as whipping cream, half and half, eggs and gelatin tend to increase the quantity. That is, the volume of the frozen mixture exceeds the volume of the prepared ingredients in its liquid state prior to freezing. This is known as *overrun* in the ice-cream industry.

When a yogurt mixture is frozen in an ice-cream maker with a dasher, air is whipped into the mixture. This increases the volume and smoothness of the final product. If the temperature of the prepared ingredients is below 40F (5C) when the freezing process begins, the yogurt mixture will freeze too quickly and a minimal amount of air will be incorporated in the frozen yogurt; thus, the volume will not increase significantly and the yogurt will probably contain large ice crystals.

About Cooking Yogurt

You may have noticed that very few mixes (prepared ingredients) in this book contain cooked yogurt. Usually other ingredients are cooked and cooled before yogurt is added. This is because yogurt is highly susceptible to curdling when heated. In cooking mixtures containing yogurt, it is very important to start cooking the mixture on very low heat and gradually increase the heat to low or medium-low. Rapid stirring of yogurt during heating also encourages curdling. So if yogurt is cooked, the basic rule is: stir gently and use low heat.

About Stirring Yogurt

You may note that most recipes in this book call for *stirred* yogurt. The reason: stirred yogurt blends more easily with other ingredients in the recipe.

About Refrigerator-Freezer Techniques

Even though you don't have an ice-cream maker, you can enjoy frozen yogurt made in the freezer compartment of your refrigerator. This method is sometimes called *Still-Freezing*. Because this method does not provide for continuous agitation of the yogurt mixture during the freezing process, the quantity and texture will vary slightly from that produced in an ice-cream maker. To produce a smoother and creamier frozen yogurt by this method, beat the prepared yogurt ingredients two or three times during the freezing process.

We recommend two techniques for doing this:

1. Food-Processor Technique. Pour prepared yogurt ingredients into an 8-inch-square baking pan; cover with foil or plastic wrap; and place in freezer compartment of refrigerator. Freeze until solid (1 to 2 hours). Break frozen mixture into pieces; spoon pieces into food processor fitted with a metal blade. Process until soft but not melted significantly. Repeat freezing and processing one or two more times, if desired.

After the final processing, stir or fold in any whole or chopped nuts, pieces of candy or cookies, large pieces of fruit, nondairy whipped topping or prepared ingredients used to produce a swirled or marbled effect. Serve after final processing or return to freezer and serve later.

2. Mixer Technique. Pour prepared yogurt ingredients into a metal mixer bowl, cover with foil or plastic wrap and place in freezer compartment of refrigerator. Freeze about 2 hours or until firm at the edges and semisoft in the center. Beat with electric mixer on medium-high speed until soft but not melted significantly. Repeat freezing and beating one or two more times, if desired.

After final beating, stir or fold in any whole or chopped nuts, pieces of candy or cookies and large pieces of fruit, nondairy whipped topping or prepared ingredients used to produce a swirled or marbled effect. Serve after final beating or return to freezer and serve later.

About Freezing Temperatures

When freezing in a brine solution (ice and salt) a good ratio of salt to ice is 2 cups salt to 8 pounds of ice cubes or crushed ice. The prepared liquid-yogurt ingredients should be at room temperature (and preferably well below) when being frozen in an ice-cream maker. If the temperature of the prepared liquid ingredients is above room temperature, it will take too long to freeze; thus requiring excessive salt and ice as well as time. On the other hand, if the prepared liquid ingredients are too cold, they will freeze too fast and will probably contain large ice crystals.

About Firming Frozen Yogurt

This process is sometimes called *hardening* or *curing* the frozen mixture. Most fans prefer to eat their frozen yogurt immediately or soon after it is made, that is, in a soft or semi-soft state. However, sometimes it is best to firm some frozen mixtures before eating them. This is especially true when an ingredient is stirred or folded in at the end of the freezing process and/or when the yogurt mixture contains ingredients with a high sugar content or alcoholic beverages, which will inhibit the freezing process.

If the prepared yogurt mixture is frozen in an ice-cream maker, follow the manufacturer's directions for firming ice cream or frozen yogurt. Regardless of the freezing process used, the frozen mixture can be firmed in the freezer compartment of a refrigerator. Simply spoon the soft frozen mixture into a chilled container with a tight-fitting lid. Place the container or containers in the refrigerator-freezer for 1 to 2 hours or until the frozen yogurt reaches the consistency you desire for serving.

About Softening Frozen Yogurt

If homemade frozen yogurt is stored in a refrigerator-freezer, it will no doubt become significantly harder than its commercial counterpart. This is because homemade frozen yogurt contains few or none of the stabilizers found in commercial products. Check the firmness of the frozen yogurt about 1 hour before serving time. If too hard, raise the temperature of the freezer compartment. This is difficult to do if you don't have a thermometer that will measure temperatures in the freezing range.

The most practical way to soften frozen yogurt is to place the container in the refrigerator 15 to 20 minutes before serving time. The quickest way to soften hard frozen yogurt is to process it in a food processor fitted with a metal blade until fluffy but not thawed. You can also spoon the hard frozen yogurt into a chilled mixer bowl and beat on medium-high speed until fluffy but not thawed.

About Storing Frozen Yogurt

If stored in a refrigerator-freezer, frozen yogurt should be placed in an airtight container. This is especially important if the freezer is a frost-free one. The process that removes moisture from the freezer compartment also removes moisture from improperly or poorly protected foods. Some quart and pint yogurt containers are excellent for storing frozen yogurt. Such containers should be made of relatively thick but pliable plastic, have a tight-fitting lid and be thoroughly washed, rinsed and dried before use.

Do not store frozen yogurt in a glass container. Frozen yogurt is best when stored at about 15F (-10C). At this temperature most frozen yogurts will be firm but pliable enough to dip and serve. Press a piece of plastic film against the exposed surface of the frozen yogurt before the lid is attached to the container. This provides a better seal against moisture being removed from the yogurt by your refrigerator's frost-free feature. Without this extra seal, the surface of the yogurt will dry out. And the plastic minimizes the formation of ice crystals in the yogurt.

About Serving Portions

6 to 8 servings per quart is about right for adults; for teens, 4 to 5 servings per quart is more realistic.

About the Recipes in This Book

All recipes were tested with the ingredients indicated. We used lowfat or nonfat milk and yogurt almost exclusively. If you substitute one kind of milk or yogurt for another, you can expect a slightly different product. For example, a richer dairy product will result in a slightly smoother and more creamy frozen product. In most cases, we feature plain (unflavored) yogurt because it is more compatible with fresh and frozen fruits as well as with traditional frozen-dessert flavors such as vanilla and chocolate.

All ingredients are listed as they appear on product labels. In a few cases, we indicated actual brand names so you would know the exact product used in testing the recipes.

Nutritional information is based on ingredients listed as a first choice. Optional choices are not included in the nutritional chart. Serving portions are 8 per quart.

Documentation

Nutrient analysis of all recipes was calculated using The Food Processor II Nutrition & Diet Analysis System software program, version 3.0, copyright 1988, 1990, by ESHA Research. It has a data base of 2400 foods and 30 nutrients and uses USDA and other scientific sources as the data source. Additionally, nutritional data provided by food manufacturers was used for some specialty items such as the candies.

Abbreviations

Because words such as *carbohydrates* are too long to fit across the bottom of the recipe in a chart form, we have abbreviated as follows:

   Cal = Calories
  Prot = Protein
 Carb = Carbohydrates
   Fib = Fiber
 Chol = Cholesterol

Vanilla

Basic Vanilla Frozen Yogurt

Traditional Vanilla Frozen Yogurt

Frozen Vanilla Supreme

Low-Cholesterol Vanilla Frozen Yogurt

Crème Brûlée Frozen Yogurt

Basic Vanilla Frozen Yogurt

So smooth you'll swear it's loaded with rich cream.

2/3 cup sugar

2 teaspoons cornstarch

1 (12-oz.) can evaporated lowfat milk

1 egg, slightly beaten

2 tablespoons light corn syrup

2 teaspoons vanilla extract

1-1/2 cups plain lowfat yogurt, stirred

In medium saucepan, combine sugar and cornstarch. Stir in milk, beaten egg and corn syrup. Cook and stir over low heat until mixture is thickened and coats a metal spoon. Remove from heat; cool. Stir in vanilla and yogurt. Freeze in ice-cream maker according to manufacturer's directions; or follow refrigerator-freezer instructions on page 4. Makes about 1 quart.

1 serving contains:

Cal	Prot	Carb	Fib	Fat	Chol	Sodium
150	6g	29g	0	1g	30mg	90mg

Traditional Vanilla Frozen Yogurt

A handy recipe to use as the base for exotic frozen drinks, favorite sundaes and other soda-fountain treats.

1-1/2 cups lowfat milk

1 teaspoon unflavored gelatin

1/2 cup sugar

3 tablespoons light corn syrup

1-1/2 teaspoons vanilla extract

1-1/2 cups plain lowfat yogurt

In small saucepan, combine milk and gelatin; let stand 1 minute. Stir over low heat until gelatin dissolves. Combine with sugar, corn syrup and vanilla. Stir in yogurt. Freeze in ice-cream maker according to manufacturer's directions; or follow refrigerator-freezer instructions on page 4. Makes about 1 quart.

1 serving contains:

Cal	Prot	Carb	Fib	Fat	Chol	Sodium
117	4g	23g	0	.1g	5mg	57mg

Frozen Vanilla Supreme

Beaten egg white gives it a light, yet creamy texture without adding any cholesterol.

1/2 cup lowfat milk

1 teaspoon unflavored gelatin

3/4 cup sugar

1-1/2 teaspoons vanilla extract

1-1/2 cups plain lowfat yogurt, stirred

1 egg white

1/3 cup water

1/3 cup nonfat dry milk

In small saucepan, combine lowfat milk and gelatin; let stand 1 minute. Cook and stir over low heat until gelatin dissolves; cool. In medium bowl, combine sugar, vanilla and yogurt; stir in dissolved gelatin mixture. In another medium bowl, combine egg white, water and nonfat dry milk. Beat until stiff but not dry. Fold into yogurt mixture. Freeze in ice-cream maker according to manufacturer's directions; or follow refrigerator-freezer instructions on page 4. Makes about 1 quart.

1 serving contains:

Cal	Prot	Carb	Fib	Fat	Chol	Sodium
122	5g	24g	0	1g	4mg	61mg

Low-Cholesterol Vanilla Frozen Yogurt

A basic vanilla frozen yogurt for those watching their cholesterol.

1-1/2 cups nonfat or lowfat milk

2/3 cup sugar

2 tablespoons light corn syrup

1 (8-oz.) carton egg substitute (Egg Beaters®), thawed

1-1/2 teaspoons vanilla extract

1 cup plain nonfat or lowfat yogurt, stirred

In 2-quart saucepan, combine milk, sugar and corn syrup. Add egg substitute; stir until well blended. Cook and stir over moderate heat until mixture is very thick. Remove from heat; cool. Add vanilla and yogurt. Freeze in ice-cream maker according to manufacturer's directions; or follow refrigerator-freezer instructions on page 4. Makes about 1 quart.

1 serving made with nonfat milk and nonfat yogurt contains:

Cal	Prot	Carb	Fib	Fat	Chol	Sodium
158	7g	26g	0	3g	2mg	108mg

1 serving made with lowfat milk and lowfat yogurt contains:

Cal	Prot	Carb	Fib	Fat	Chol	Sodium
161	6g	26g	0	4g	4mg	102mg

Crème Brûlée Frozen Yogurt

For holiday entertaining this recipe makes excellent Eggnog Frozen Yogurt. Simply substitute a light dusting of ground nutmeg for the Brûlée Topping. This recipe also provides an excellent eggnog drink when cooked and chilled, but not frozen.

Brûlée Topping:

1/3 cup lightly packed brown sugar

1 tablespoon orange liqueur

1 or 2 dashes ground cloves

Frozen Yogurt:

1-1/4 cups nonfat milk

3 beaten eggs or 6 oz. egg substitute (Egg Beaters®), thawed

3/4 cup granulated sugar

1/8 teaspoon ground cinnamon

1/4 teaspoon salt, optional

2 teaspoons vanilla extract

1-1/4 cups plain nonfat yogurt, stirred

Brûlée Topping: In small bowl, break up any brown sugar lumps with a fork or spoon. Add liqueur and cloves; mix thoroughly. Refrigerate in covered container until consumed.

Frozen Yogurt: In 1-1/2-quart heavy saucepan, combine milk, eggs, granulated sugar, cinnamon and salt, if desired. Cook and stir over low heat 10 minutes or until mixture thickens and coats a metal spoon. Remove from heat; cool. Stir in vanilla and yogurt. Freeze in ice-cream maker according to manufacturer's directions; or follow refrigerator-freezer instructions on page 4. Sprinkle topping over each serving. Makes about 1 quart.

1 serving made with eggs contains:

Cal	Prot	Carb	Fib	Fat	Chol	Sodium
167	6g	32g	0	2g	79mg	76mg

1 serving made with egg substitute contains:

Cal	Prot	Carb	Fib	Fat	Chol	Sodium
173	6g	33g	0	3g	2mg	94mg

Chocolate

Creamy Chocolate Frozen Yogurt

Sugar-Free Milk Chocolate Special

Chocolate Rocky Road Frozen Yogurt

Irish Cream Frozen Yogurt

Chocolate Delight Frozen Yogurt

Frosty Bahia Blend

Chocolate Fleck Frozen Yogurt

Toasted Almond Fudge Frozen Yogurt

Chocolate Peanut Butter Banana Treat

Sicilian Cheesecake Frozen Yogurt

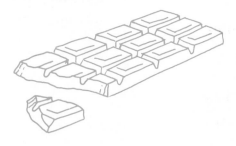

Creamy Chocolate Frozen Yogurt

Everyone's favorite flavor made with ever-popular chocolate syrup.

2 teaspoons cornstarch

1/2 cup sugar

1 (12-oz.) can evaporated skimmed or evaporated lowfat milk

1 egg, slightly beaten

2/3 cup chocolate syrup

1/2 teaspoon vanilla extract

1 cup plain lowfat yogurt, stirred

In medium saucepan, combine cornstarch and sugar. Stir in milk and egg. Cook and stir over low heat 6 to 8 minutes or until mixture coats a metal spoon. Remove from heat. Add chocolate syrup and cool. Stir in vanilla and yogurt. Freeze in ice-cream maker according to manufacturer's directions; or follow refrigerator-freezer instructions on page 4. Makes about 1 quart.

1 serving contains:

Cal	Prot	Carb	Fib	Fat	Chol	Sodium
172	7g	35g	0	2g	30mg	104mg

Sugar-Free Milk-Chocolate Special

It's not necessary to add any sugar to this recipe when you use Equal® as a sweetener.

1/2 cup lowfat milk

1 teaspoon unflavored gelatin

1/2 cup chocolate-flavored syrup

1 cup plain lowfat yogurt, stirred

4 (1-gram) packets Equal®

1/2 teaspoon vanilla extract

1 egg white

1/3 cup water

1/3 cup nonfat dry milk

In small saucepan, combine 1/2 cup lowfat milk and gelatin; let stand 1 minute. Stir over low heat until gelatin dissolves; set aside. In small bowl, stir chocolate syrup into yogurt. Add Equal and vanilla. In medium bowl, combine egg white, water and nonfat dry milk. Beat until stiff peaks form. Fold into chocolate mixture. Freeze in ice-cream maker according to manufacturer's directions; or follow refrigerator-freezer instructions on page 4. Makes about 1 quart.

1 serving contains:

Cal	Prot	Carb	Fib	Fat	Chol	Sodium
83	5g	15g	1g	1g	3mg	66mg

Chocolate Rocky Road Frozen Yogurt

Irresistible temptation of chocolate yogurt that's studded with chunks of marshmallows and nuts.

1/4 cup unsweetened cocoa powder

2 teaspoons cornstarch

3/4 cup sugar

1-1/4 cups lowfat milk

1-1/2 cups plain lowfat yogurt, stirred

1/2 teaspoon vanilla extract

1/2 cup miniature marshmallows, halved*

1/4 cup chopped pecans or walnuts*

*If this recipe will be frozen in a refrigerator freezer, see page 4 or 5 before adding these ingredients.

In medium saucepan, combine cocoa powder, cornstarch and sugar. Stir in milk. Cook and stir over moderate heat until mixture simmers and is slightly thickened. Remove from heat; cool. Stir in yogurt, vanilla, marshmallows and nuts. Freeze in ice-cream maker according to manufacturer's directions; or follow refrigerator-freezer instructions on page 4. Makes about 1 quart.

1 serving contains:

Cal	Prot	Carb	Fib	Fat	Chol	Sodium
194	5g	38g	1g	4g	4mg	63mg

Irish Cream Frozen Yogurt

A touch of Irish Cream teams up with chocolate for a mouth-watering change of pace.

2 tablespoons water

1 teaspoon unflavored gelatin

3 oz. semi-sweet chocolate, coarsely chopped

3/4 cup lowfat milk

1/4 cup light corn syrup

1/4 cup sugar

3 tablespoons Bailey's Irish Cream® liqueur

1 cup plain lowfat yogurt, stirred

1 egg white

1/3 cup water

1/3 cup nonfat dry milk

In small saucepan, combine 2 tablespoons water and gelatin; let stand 1 minute. Stir over low heat until gelatin dissolves; set aside. In medium saucepan, combine chocolate, milk, corn syrup and sugar. Cook and whisk over low heat until mixture is smooth. Stir in dissolved gelatin mixture; cool. Add Irish cream and yogurt. Beat egg white, 1/3 cup water and non-fat dry milk until stiff but not dry. Fold into yogurt mixture. Freeze in ice-cream maker according to manufacturer's directions; or follow refrigerator-freezer instructions on page 4. Makes about 1 quart.

1 serving contains:

Cal	Prot	Carb	Fib	Fat	Chol	Sodium
169	5g	26g	1g	5g	3mg	66mg

Chocolate Delight Frozen Yogurt

Hard to believe this smooth, rich-tasting treat is made with an egg substitute.

1/4 cup unsweetened cocoa powder

3/4 cup sugar

1 (12-oz.) can evaporated skimmed or evaporated lowfat milk

1 (8-oz.) carton egg substitute (Egg Beaters®), thawed

1/2 teaspoon vanilla extract

1 cup plain yogurt, stirred

In medium saucepan, combine cocoa and sugar. Add milk and egg substitute. Whisk until smooth. Cook and whisk over moderate heat until mixture is very thick; cool. Stir in vanilla and yogurt. Freeze in ice-cream maker according to manufacturer's directions; or follow refrigerator-freezer instructions on page 4. Makes about 1 quart.

1 serving contains:

Cal	Prot	Carb	Fib	Fat	Chol	Sodium
183	9g	28g	1g	4g	4mg	136mg

Frosty Bahia Blend

A triple-flavor treat borrowed from our South-American friends.

2 tablespoons water

1 teaspoon unflavored gelatin

3 oz. semi-sweet chocolate, coarsely chopped

1-1/2 cups lowfat milk

1/4 teaspoon ground cinnamon

2 teaspoons instant-coffee crystals

3/4 cup sugar

1 cup plain lowfat yogurt, stirred

In measuring cup, combine water and gelatin; set aside. In medium saucepan, combine chocolate, milk, cinnamon, coffee crystals and sugar. Cook and stir over medium-low heat until chocolate melts. Remove from heat; stir in softened gelatin. Cool; then add yogurt. Freeze in ice-cream maker according to manufacturer's directions; or follow refrigerator-freezer instructions on page 4. Makes about 1 quart.

1 serving contains:

Cal	Prot	Carb	Fib	Fat	Chol	Sodium
168	4g	29g	1g	5g	4mg	46mg

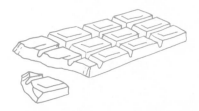

Chocolate Fleck Frozen Yogurt

When melted chocolate contacts cold yogurt, it breaks into thin chips to provide that great flavor.

3/4 cup sugar

2 teaspoons cornstarch

1 (12-oz.) can lowfat evaporated milk

1 teaspoon vanilla extract

1 cup plain lowfat yogurt, stirred

2 oz. semi-sweet chocolate

In medium saucepan, combine sugar and cornstarch. Stir in milk. Cook and stir over moderate heat until thickened and bubbly. Remove from heat; cool to luke-warm. Add vanilla and yogurt. Refrigerate until mixture is cold. Melt chocolate. While chocolate is hot, pour it very slowly into chilled yogurt mixture while stirring gently. Freeze in ice-cream maker according to manufacturer's directions; or follow refrigerator-freezer instructions on page 4. Makes about 1 quart.

1 serving contains:

Cal	Prot	Carb	Fib	Fat	Chol	Sodium
162	5g	30g	0	3g	3mg	70mg

Toasted Almond Fudge Frozen Yogurt

Blanched almonds toast well in a 375F (190C) oven for 6 to 8 minutes or until light tan.

3/4 cup granulated sugar

3 tablespoons unsweetened cocoa powder

1/4 teaspoon salt, optional

1-1/4 cups nonfat milk

1 tablespoon light corn syrup

1 tablespoon margarine or butter, optional

1 teaspoon vanilla extract

1/2 cup coarsely chopped, toasted blanched almonds*

1/3 cup nonfat milk

1 tablespoon nonfat dry milk

1 tablespoon powdered sugar

1-1/4 cups plain nonfat yogurt, stirred

*If this recipe will be frozen in a refrigerator freezer, see page 4 or 5 before adding this ingredient.

In 1-1/2-quart saucepan, combine 3/4 cup granulated sugar, cocoa powder, salt (if desired), 1-1/4 cups nonfat milk and corn syrup. Add margarine or butter, if desired. Simmer over medium-low heat, stirring frequently for 8 to 10 minutes. Remove from heat; stir in vanilla and toasted almonds. Cool. In bowl, combine 1/3 cup nonfat milk and nonfat dry milk; stir until dry milk dissolves. Place beater in bowl with milk. Freeze in refrigerator-freezer until ice crystals form around edge of milk (about 30 minutes). Remove mixer bowl and beaters from freezer; beat with electric mixer on medium speed until soft peaks form. Add powdered sugar and continue beating on high speed until stiff peaks form. Stir yogurt into cooled cocoa mixture. Fold in whipped milk. Freeze in ice-cream maker according to manufacturer's directions; or follow refrigerator-freezer instructions on page 4. Makes about 1 quart.

1 serving contains:

Cal	Prot	Carb	Fib	Fat	Chol	Sodium
179	6g	29g	2g	5g	2mg	58mg

Chocolate Peanut Butter Banana Treat

A magical, mouth-watering combination of nostalgic go-togethers.

1/4 cup crunchy peanut butter

2 oz. semi-sweet chocolate, melted

1 medium banana, peeled and mashed

1 (12-oz.) can evaporated lowfat milk

1/2 cup sugar

1/2 teaspoon vanilla extract

1 cup plain lowfat yogurt, stirred

In medium bowl, combine peanut butter, melted chocolate and banana. Add evaporated milk, sugar and vanilla. Stir in yogurt. Freeze in ice-cream maker according to manufacturer's directions; or follow refrigerator-freezer instructions on page 4. Makes about 1 quart.

1 serving contains:

Cal	Prot	Carb	Fib	Fat	Chol	Sodium
196	7g	28g	1g	7g	3mg	103mg

Sicilian Cheesecake Frozen Yogurt

We borrowed Mediterranean flavor combinations for this unusual dessert.

3 oz. semi-sweet chocolate, coarsely chopped

2 eggs, slightly beaten

2/3 cup lowfat milk

3/4 cup cottage cheese

1/2 cup sugar

1 tablespoon rum or rum flavoring

1 cup plain lowfat yogurt, stirred

1/3 cup chopped candied fruits*

*If this recipe will be frozen in a refrigerator freezer, see page 4 or 5 before adding this ingredient.

In medium saucepan, combine chocolate, eggs and milk. Cook and stir over low heat until chocolate melts; remove from heat. In blender or food processor fitted with metal blade, purée cottage cheese and sugar. Add to chocolate mixture; stir until smooth. Cool; then add rum, yogurt and fruits. Freeze in ice-cream maker according to manufacturer's directions; or follow refrigerator-freezer instructions on page 4. Makes about 1 quart.

1 serving contains:

Cal	Prot	Carb	Fib	Fat	Chol	Sodium
200	7g	30g	0	7g	58mg	155mg

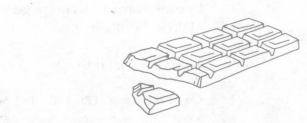

Berries

Heavenly Strawberry Frozen Yogurt

Lite Strawberry Frozen Yogurt

Low-Sugar Strawberry Yogurt

Strawberry Smoothie

Rich Strawberry Frozen Yogurt

Favorite Raspberry Frozen Yogurt

Raspberry Frozen Yogurt

Raspberry Applesauce Mallow

Sugar-Free Raspberry Frozen Yogurt

Berry Grower's Blackberry Frozen Yogurt

Frozen Boysenberry Supreme

Boysenberry Cassis Frozen Yogurt

Crunchy Blackberry Frozen Yogurt

White Chocolate Blackberry Swirl

Blueberry Ripple Frozen Yogurt

Blueberry Rocky Road Frozen Yogurt

Orange Blueberry Frozen Yogurt

Heavenly Strawberry Frozen Yogurt

A dreamy pink frozen dessert that goes together with little effort.

1 cup lowfat milk

1 (1.3-oz.) envelope Dream Whip® whipped topping mix

2/3 cup sugar

1 cup fresh or frozen unsweetened strawberries

1 cup plain lowfat yogurt, stirred

In medium mixing bowl, combine milk and whipped topping mix; stir until well mixed. Add sugar. In blender or food processor fitted with metal blade, process berries until finely chopped. Add to topping mixture. Stir in yogurt. Freeze in ice-cream maker according to manufacturer's directions; or follow refrigerator-freezer instructions on page 4. Makes about 1 quart.

1 serving contains:

Cal	Prot	Carb	Fib	Fat	Chol	Sodium
127	3g	24g	0	3g	3mg	42mg

Lite Strawberry Frozen Yogurt

A very smooth and creamy dessert that's low in fat and cholesterol.

1/4 cup nonfat milk

2 tablespoons nonfat dry milk

1 tablespoon sugar

1 teaspoon unflavored gelatin

2/3 cup nonfat milk

**1 cup fresh or frozen
unsweetened strawberries**

2/3 cup sugar

1/2 teaspoon vanilla extract

**1 cup nonfat plain yogurt,
stirred**

In small mixer bowl, combine 1/4 cup nonfat milk with nonfat dry milk; stir until dry milk dissolves. Place mixer bowl and beaters in refrigerator-freezer until ice crystals begin to form around edge of milk (about 30 minutes). Remove mixer bowl and beaters from freezer; beat at high speed until soft peaks form. Continue beating while adding 1 tablespoon sugar until stiff peaks form; refrigerate. In small saucepan, sprinkle gelatin over 2/3 cup milk; let stand 1 minute. Cook and stir over very low heat just until gelatin dissolves. Remove from heat; set aside. In blender or food processor, purée strawberries with 2/3 cup sugar until sugar dissolves. In medium bowl, combine strawberry purée, gelatin mixture, vanilla extract and yogurt. Fold whipped milk into strawberry mixture. Freeze in ice-cream maker according to manufacturer's directions; or follow refrigerator-freezer instructions on page 4. Makes about 1 quart.

1 serving contains:

Cal	Prot	Carb	Fib	Fat	Chol	Sodium
110	4g	24g	1g	0	1mg	44mg

Low-Sugar Strawberry Yogurt

Designed to help you cut back on sugar and fat.

1 cup fresh or frozen unsweetened strawberries

4 (1-gram) packets Sweet 'n Low® sweetener

1/3 cup sugar

1/2 teaspoon vanilla extract

1 cup plain lowfat yogurt, stirred

1 egg white

1/3 cup nonfat dry milk

1/3 cup cold water

In blender or food processor fitted with metal blade, combine berries, sweetener and sugar. Process until berries are finely chopped. Stir in vanilla and yogurt. In medium bowl, beat egg white, nonfat dry milk and water until stiff but not dry. Carefully fold into berry mixture until smooth. Freeze in ice-cream maker according to manufacturer's directions; or follow refrigerator-freezer instructions on page 4. Makes about 1 quart.

1 serving contains:

Cal	Prot	Carb	Fib	Fat	Chol	Sodium
68	3g	13g	0	1g	2mg	42mg

Strawberry Smoothie

The banana's texture plus a whole egg result in a surprisingly smooth frozen yogurt.

1/2 cup lowfat milk

1 egg, slightly beaten

1-1/2 cups fresh or frozen unsweetened strawberries

1 small banana, peeled and quartered

2 tablespoons light corn syrup

1/2 cup brown sugar

1/4 teaspoon vanilla extract

3/4 cup plain lowfat yogurt, stirred

In small saucepan, cook and stir milk and egg over low heat until thickened; set aside. In blender or food processor fitted with metal blade, combine strawberries, banana, corn syrup, brown sugar and vanilla. Process until finely chopped. Combine with cooked egg mixture. Stir in yogurt. Freeze in ice-cream maker according to manufacturer's directions; or follow refrigerator-freezer instructions on page 4. Makes about 1 quart.

1 serving contains:

Cal	Prot	Carb	Fib	Fat	Chol	Sodium
116	3g	25g	1g	1g	28mg	40mg

Rich Strawberry Frozen Yogurt

Cream and eggs result in a smoother, richer treat.

1/2 cup sugar

2 teaspoons cornstarch

1 cup half and half or whipping cream

1/4 cup light corn syrup

1 egg, slightly beaten

2 cups fresh or frozen unsweetened strawberries

1 cup plain lowfat yogurt, stirred

In medium saucepan, combine sugar and cornstarch; stir in half and half and corn syrup. Cook and stir over moderate heat until mixture simmers; cook 1 minute longer. Remove from heat; stir in beaten egg. Return to low heat; cook and stir 2 minutes. Remove from heat; cool. In blender or food processor fitted with metal blade, purée berries. Add to cool egg mixture; stir in yogurt. Freeze in ice-cream maker according to manufacturer's directions; or follow refrigerator-freezer instructions on page 4. Makes about 1 quart.

1 serving contains:

Cal	Prot	Carb	Fib	Fat	Chol	Sodium
157	3g	27g	1g	5g	39mg	46mg

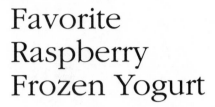

Favorite Raspberry Frozen Yogurt

Traditional ingredients combine to make a smooth and creamy berry yogurt.

2 cups fresh or frozen unsweetened raspberries

2/3 cup sugar

2 teaspoons cornstarch

1/4 cup honey

1 cup lowfat milk

1 cup plain lowfat yogurt, stirred

In blender or food processor fitted with metal blade, purée raspberries; strain and discard seeds. In medium saucepan, mix sugar and cornstarch. Stir in honey and milk. Cook and stir over low heat until mixture simmers (about 6 to 8 minutes). Remove from heat; add puréed berries. Cool; stir in yogurt. Freeze in ice-cream maker according to manufacturer's directions; or follow refrigerator-freezer instructions on page 4. Makes about 1 quart.

1 serving contains:

Cal	Prot	Carb	Fib	Fat	Chol	Sodium
145	3g	33g	2g	1g	3mg	36mg

Raspberry Frozen Yogurt

A wonderful way to have rich-tasting frozen dessert.

1 cup lowfat milk

1/2 cup sugar

3 tablespoons light corn syrup

1 (8-oz.) carton egg substitute (Egg Beaters®), thawed

2 cups fresh or frozen unsweetened raspberries

1 cup plain lowfat yogurt, stirred

In medium saucepan, combine milk, sugar and corn syrup. Stir in egg substitute; whisk until smooth. Cook and stir over moderate heat until mixture is very thick; remove from heat. In blender or food processor fitted with metal blade, purée berries; strain and discard seeds. Stir strained berries and yogurt into cooked mixture. Freeze in ice-cream maker according to manufacturer's directions; or follow refrigerator-freezer instructions on page 4. Makes about 1 quart.

1 serving contains:

Cal	Prot	Carb	Fib	Fat	Chol	Sodium
161	6g	26g	2g	4g	3mg	96mg

Raspberry Applesauce Mallow

*Let the flavors and textures blend
a while before freezing.*

**1 cup fresh or frozen
  unsweetened raspberries**

1 teaspoon unflavored gelatin

1/4 cup water

1 cup unsweetened applesauce

2/3 cup sugar

**1/2 cup miniature
  marshmallows, halved**

**1 cup plain lowfat yogurt,
  stirred**

In blender or food processor fitted with metal blade, purée raspberries. Strain and discard seeds. In small saucepan, combine gelatin and water; let stand 1 minute. Cook and stir over low heat until gelatin dissolves. Combine with puréed raspberries, applesauce, sugar and marshmallows. Stir in yogurt. Cover; refrigerate at least 1/2 hour before freezing. Freeze in ice-cream maker according to manufacturer's directions; or follow refrigerator-freezer instructions on page 4. Makes about 1 quart.

1 serving contains:

Cal	Prot	Carb	Fib	Fat	Chol	Sodium
118	3g	27g	2g	1g	2mg	25mg

Sugar-Free Raspberry Frozen Yogurt

Enjoy this great dessert without worrying about sugar.

1/4 cup water

1 teaspoon unflavored gelatin

1 cup fresh or frozen unsweetened raspberries

12 (1-gram) packets Equal®

1 cup plain lowfat yogurt, stirred

1 egg white

1/3 cup cold water

1/3 cup nonfat dry milk

In small saucepan, combine 1/4 cup water with gelatin; let stand 1 minute. Cook and stir over low heat until gelatin dissolves; set aside. In blender or food processor fitted with metal blade, purée berries. Strain; discard seeds. Combine puréed berries with Equal and dissolved gelatin. Stir in yogurt. In small bowl, combine egg white with 1/3 cup water and dry milk; beat until stiff but not dry. Fold into raspberry mixture. Freeze in ice-cream maker according to manufacturer's directions; or follow refrigerator-freezer instructions on page 4. Makes about 1 quart.

1 serving contains:

Cal	Prot	Carb	Fib	Fat	Chol	Sodium
42	4g	5g	1g	1g	2mg	43mg

Berry Grower's Blackberry Frozen Yogurt

Combining cornstarch with honey results in a smoother textured frozen yogurt.

2 cups fresh or frozen unsweetened blackberries or boysenberries

2/3 cup sugar

2 teaspoons cornstarch

2 tablespoons honey

1 cup lowfat milk

1 cup plain lowfat yogurt, stirred

In blender or food processor fitted with metal blade, purée berries; strain and discard seeds. Set purée aside. In small saucepan, combine sugar and cornstarch. Stir in honey and milk. Cook and stir over medium heat until translucent (about 5 to 7 minutes). Stir in puréed berries. Cool; then add yogurt. Freeze in ice-cream maker according to manufacturer's directions; or follow refrigerator-freezer instructions on page 4. Makes about 1 quart.

1 serving contains:

Cal	Prot	Carb	Fib	Fat	Chol	Sodium
132	3g	30g	2g	1g	3mg	36mg

Frozen Boysenberry Supreme

One of our favorites: creamy, yet light-textured with a refreshing berry flavor.

2/3 cup sugar

2 teaspoons cornstarch

3/4 cup evaporated skimmed milk

1 egg, slightly beaten

2 tablespoons light corn syrup

2 cups fresh or frozen unsweetened boysenberries

1 cup plain lowfat yogurt, stirred

In medium saucepan, combine sugar and cornstarch. Stir in milk, beaten egg and corn syrup. Cook and stir over low heat until mixture coats metal spoon and is slightly thickened; set aside. In blender or food processor fitted with metal blade, purée berries. Strain and discard seeds. Add to cooked mixture. Stir in yogurt. Freeze in ice-cream maker according to manufacturer's directions; or follow refrigerator-freezer instructions on page 4. Makes about 1 quart.

1 serving contains:

Cal	Prot	Carb	Fib	Fat	Chol	Sodium
143	4g	30g	1g	1g	29mg	59mg

Boysenberry Cassis Frozen Yogurt

If frozen berries are used, thaw them before puréeing.

2 cups fresh or frozen unsweetened boysenberries or blackberries

1 teaspoon unflavored gelatin

1/2 cup lowfat milk

1/3 cup sugar

3 tablespoons Cassis black-currant liqueur

1/4 cup light corn syrup

1-1/2 cups plain lowfat yogurt, stirred

In blender or food processor fitted with metal blade, purée berries; strain and discard seeds. Set aside berry purée. In medium saucepan, sprinkle gelatin over milk; let stand 1 minute. Cook and stir over low heat until gelatin dissolves. Add sugar, Cassis, corn syrup and puréed berries; cool. Stir in yogurt. Freeze in ice-cream maker according to manufacturer's directions; or follow refrigerator-freezer instructions on page 4. Makes about 1 quart.

1 serving contains:

Cal	Prot	Carb	Fib	Fat	Chol	Sodium
114	4g	24g	2g	1g	3mg	44mg

Crunchy Blackberry Frozen Yogurt

Stir in the granola after berry mixture is frozen so you'll have a contrast of crunchy and smooth textures.

2 cups fresh or frozen unsweetened blackberries or boysenberries

1 teaspoon unflavored gelatin

1/4 cup water

2/3 cup sugar

1/4 cup honey

1/2 cup apple juice

1 cup plain lowfat yogurt, stirred

1/2 cup granola

In blender or food processor fitted with metal blade, purée berries; strain and discard seeds. In small saucepan, sprinkle gelatin over water; let stand 1 minute. Cook and stir over low heat until gelatin dissolves. Combine with sugar, honey, apple juice, puréed berries and yogurt. Freeze in ice-cream maker according to manufacturer's directions. When frozen, stir in granola. Or follow refrigerator-freezer instructions on page 4 and stir in granola after the final processing or beating. Makes about 1 quart.

1 serving contains:

Cal	Prot	Carb	Fib	Fat	Chol	Sodium
176	4g	38g	3g	2g	2mg	37mg

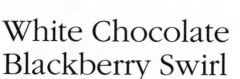

White Chocolate Blackberry Swirl

Use the coarse side of shredder or swivel-blade vegetable peeler to make thin strips of white chocolate.

2 cups fresh or frozen unsweetened blackberries or boysenberries

1 teaspoon unflavored gelatin

1/4 cup water

2/3 cup sugar

2/3 cup lowfat milk

1 cup plain lowfat yogurt, stirred

4 oz. white baking bar or white chocolate candy bar, coarsely shredded*

*If this recipe will be frozen in a refrigerator freezer, please see page 4 or 5 before adding this ingredient.

In blender or food processor fitted with metal blade, purée berries. Strain and discard seeds; set purée aside. In small sauce-pan, sprinkle gelatin over water; let stand 1 minute. Cook and stir over low heat until gelatin dissolves. Stir in sugar, milk, puréed berries and yogurt. Then fold in shredded white chocolate. Freeze in ice-cream maker accord-ing to manufacturer's directions; or follow refrigerator-freezer instructions on page 4. Makes about 1 quart.

1 serving contains:

Cal	Prot	Carb	Fib	Fat	Chol	Sodium
194	4g	32g	3g	6g	3mg	47mg

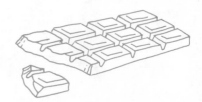

Blueberry Ripple Frozen Yogurt

This frozen yogurt stores well for several days in a refrigerator freezer.

1 cup fresh or frozen unsweetened blueberries

1/4 cup sugar

1/2 teaspoon lemon juice

2/3 cup sugar

2 teaspoons cornstarch

1-1/2 cups nonfat milk

1-1/2 cups plain nonfat yogurt, stirred

2 teaspoons vanilla extract

In blender or food processor fitted with metal blade, purée blueberries, 1/4 cup sugar and lemon juice. Refrigerate purée while preparing remaining ingredients. In 1-quart saucepan, combine 2/3 cup sugar and cornstarch. Then stir in milk. Cook over low heat, stirring frequently, until mixture simmers. Simmer about 2 minutes; remove from heat and cool. Stir in yogurt and vanilla. Freeze in ice-cream maker according to manufacturer's directions. When frozen stir in refrigerated blueberry mixture just enough to create a rippled effect. Or follow refrigerator-freezer instructions on page 4; and after final processing or beating, stir in refrigerated blueberry mixture just enough to create a rippled effect. Makes about 1 quart.

1 serving contains:

Cal	Prot	Carb	Fib	Fat	Chol	Sodium
141	4g	32g	0	0	2mg	58mg

Blueberry Rocky Road Frozen Yogurt

Chunks of miniature marshmallows contribute a surprise texture and flavor contrast.

2 cups fresh or unsweetened frozen blueberries

1/2 cup orange juice

1 teaspoon unflavored gelatin

1/4 cup water

1/4 teaspoon grated orange peel

2 tablespoons honey

1/4 cup sugar

1/2 cup miniature marshmallows, halved*

1 cup plain lowfat yogurt, stirred

*If this recipe will be frozen in a refrigerator freezer, see page 4 or 5 before adding this ingredient.

In blender or food processor fitted with metal blade, finely chop blueberries with orange juice; set aside. In small saucepan, sprinkle gelatin over water; let stand 1 minute. Cook and stir over low heat until gelatin dissolves. Remove from heat; add orange peel, honey, sugar, puréed berry mixture, marshmallows and yogurt. Freeze in ice-cream maker according to manufacturer's directions; or follow refrigerator-freezer instructions on page 4. Makes about 1 quart.

1 serving contains:

Cal	Prot	Carb	Fib	Fat	Chol	Sodium
101	3g	22g	1g	1g	2mg	27mg

Orange Blueberry Frozen Yogurt

Its beautiful pale-purple color is accented with dark flecks of blueberries.

1/2 cup lowfat milk

1 teaspoon unflavored gelatin

1/2 cup sugar

2 tablespoons honey

2 (1" x 1/4") strips of orange peel

1-1/2 cups fresh or frozen unsweetened blueberries

1/4 cup orange juice

3/4 cup plain lowfat yogurt, stirred

In small saucepan, combine milk and gelatin; let stand 1 minute. Add sugar, honey and orange peel. Cook and stir over low heat until gelatin dissolves. Remove from heat; cool. In blender or food processor fitted with metal blade, purée berries with orange juice. Remove and discard orange peel from gelatin mixture. Combine berry purée, gelatin mixture and yogurt. Freeze in ice-cream maker according to manufacturer's directions; or follow refrigerator-freezer instructions on page 4. Makes about 1 quart.

1 serving contains:

Cal	Prot	Carb	Fib	Fat	Chol	Sodium
107	3g	24g	1g	1g	2mg	26mg

Orchard Fruits

Rich Peach Frozen Yogurt

Peach Frozen Yogurt with Sweet 'n Low®

Peachy Almond Frozen Yogurt

Yankee Peach Frozen Yogurt

Frozen Peach Macaroon Crumble

Creamy Melba Freeze

Peach Cobbler Frozen Yogurt

Toasted Almond Nectarine Frozen Yogurt

Sugar-Free Nectarine Frozen Yogurt

Orchard-Fresh Plum Frozen Yogurt

Spicy Plum Frozen Yogurt

Bit O' Gold Plum Frozen Yogurt

Nutty Plum Frozen Yogurt

Burgundy Plum Frozen Yogurt

Fresh Apricot Frozen Yogurt

Anytime Apricot Honey Frozen Yogurt

Cherry-Berry Frozen Yogurt

Port 'O Pear Frozen Yogurt

A Taste of Autumn

Red-Hot Apple Frozen Yogurt

Maple Apple Frozen Yogurt

Rich Peach Frozen Yogurt

Rich, smooth and easy to make.

1/2 cup sugar

1 cup half and half or whipping cream

2 eggs, slightly beaten

1/4 cup light corn syrup

3 ripe medium peaches, peeled and quartered

1/8 teaspoon almond extract

1/2 cup plain lowfat yogurt, stirred

In medium saucepan, combine sugar, half and half or whipping cream, eggs and corn syrup. Cook and stir over low heat until mixture thickens and coats a metal spoon. Remove from heat; cool. In blender or food processor fitted with metal blade, process peaches until almost smooth. Add peach and almond extract to cooled egg mixture. Stir in yogurt. Freeze in ice-cream maker according to manufacturer's directions; or follow refrigerator-freezer instructions on page 4. Makes about 1 quart.

1 serving contains:

Cal	Prot	Carb	Fib	Fat	Chol	Sodium
157	3g	26g	1g	5g	64mg	44mg

Peach Frozen Yogurt with Sweet 'n Low®

It takes about one-half the usual amount of sugar when using Sweet 'n Low®.

1/4 cup lowfat milk

1 teaspoon unflavored gelatin

2 ripe medium-large peaches, peeled and coarsely chopped

5 (1-gram) packets Sweet 'n Low® sweetener

1/3 cup sugar

1/2 teaspoon vanilla extract

1 cup plain lowfat yogurt, stirred

1 egg white

1/3 cup nonfat dry milk

1/3 cup cold water

In small saucepan, combine 1/4 cup milk and gelatin; let stand 1 minute. Cook and stir over low heat until gelatin dissolves. Remove from heat; set aside. In blender or food processor fitted with metal blade, combine peaches, sweetener and sugar. Process until fruit is finely chopped. Stir in vanilla, dissolved gelatin and yogurt. In medium bowl, beat egg white, dry milk and water until stiff but not dry. Fold into peach mixture. Freeze in ice-cream maker according to manufacturer's directions; or follow refrigerator-freezer instructions on page 4. Makes about 1 quart.

1 serving contains:

Cal	Prot	Carb	Fib	Fat	Chol	Sodium
78	4g	15g	1g	1g	3mg	47mg

Peachy Almond Frozen Yogurt

Almond paste contributes just the right accent to fresh peaches.

3 ripe medium peaches, peeled and sliced

2 tablespoons almond paste

1/2 cup sugar

3/4 cup evaporated lowfat milk

1 cup plain lowfat yogurt, stirred

In blender or food processor fitted with metal blade, combine peaches, almond paste and sugar. Process until peaches are finely chopped. Stir in milk and yogurt. Freeze in ice-cream maker according to manufacturer's directions; or follow refrigerator-freezer instructions on page 4. Makes about 1 quart.

1 serving contains:

Cal	Prot	Carb	Fib	Fat	Chol	Sodium
115	4g	22g	1g	1g	3mg	48mg

Yankee Peach Frozen Yogurt

A palate perk-up for maple-flavor fans.

3 ripe large peaches, peeled and chopped

1/4 cup sugar

1 teaspoon unflavored gelatin

1/2 cup lowfat milk

1/3 cup maple-flavored syrup

1 cup plain lowfat yogurt, stirred

In blender or food processor fitted with metal blade, combine peaches and sugar. Process until peaches are finely chopped but not puréed. Pour into medium bowl. In small saucepan, sprinkle gelatin over milk; let stand 1 minute. Cook and stir over low heat until gelatin dissolves. Add to chopped peach mixture; then stir in maple syrup and yogurt. Freeze in ice-cream maker according to manufacturer's directions; or follow refrigerator-freezer instructions on page 4. Makes about 1 quart.

1 serving contains:

Cal	Prot	Carb	Fib	Fat	Chol	Sodium
100	3g	21g	1g	1g	2mg	31mg

Frozen Peach Macaroon Crumble

Crumbled macaroons enhance the taste in addition to providing a welcomed crunch to this yogurt.

1/2 cup lowfat milk

1 teaspoon unflavored gelatin

1/2 cup sugar

1/8 cup light corn syrup

1/8 teaspoon ground nutmeg

4 ripe medium peaches, peeled and sliced

3/4 cup plain lowfat yogurt, stirred

4 (2-inch-diameter) crisp macaroon cookies, coarsely crumbled*

*If this recipe will be frozen in a refrigerator freezer, see page 4 or 5 before adding this ingredient.

In small saucepan, combine milk and gelatin; let stand 1 minute. Cook and stir over low heat until gelatin dissolves. Remove from heat. Stir in sugar, corn syrup and nutmeg; set aside. In blender or food processor fitted with metal blade, finely chop peaches. In medium bowl, combine peaches and gelatin mixture; stir in yogurt. Freeze in ice-cream maker according to manufacturer's directions. When frozen fold in crumbled macaroons. Or follow refrigerator-freezer instructions on page 4. Makes about 1 quart.

1 serving contains:

Cal	Prot	Carb	Fib	Fat	Chol	Sodium
133	3g	28g	1g	1g	2mg	36mg

Creamy Melba Freeze

A quick and easy combination that results in a smooth frozen dessert.

1 cup fresh or frozen unsweetened raspberries

2 ripe medium peaches, peeled and sliced

1 teaspoon lemon juice

3/4 cup plain lowfat yogurt, stirred

1 (14-oz.) can sweetened condensed milk

In blender or food processor fitted with metal blade, combine raspberries, peaches and lemon juice. Process until fruit is finely chopped. In medium bowl, combine yogurt and condensed milk. Gradually stir in fruit mixture. Freeze in ice-cream maker according to manufacturer's directions; or follow refrigerator-freezer instructions on page 4. Makes about 1 quart.

1 serving contains:

Cal	Prot	Carb	Fib	Fat	Chol	Sodium
190	5g	33g	1g	5g	18mg	78mg

Peach Cobbler Frozen Yogurt

Macaroons make a good substitute for vanilla wafers.

2 large or 3 medium fresh peaches, peeled and sliced (about 2-1/2 cups)

2 teaspoons lemon juice

3/4 cup sugar

1/2 cup nonfat milk

1 teaspoon unflavored gelatin

1/4 teaspoon ground cinnamon

1 tablespoon margarine or butter, optional

1/2 teaspoon vanilla extract

1/2 cup nonfat milk

1 cup plain nonfat yogurt, stirred

3 or 4 vanilla wafers, broken into 1/2-inch pieces

In blender or food processor fitted with metal blade, combine peaches, lemon juice and sugar. Process until chopped but not puréed. In 1-1/2- or 2-quart saucepan, combine peach mixture and 1/2 cup milk. Sprinkle gelatin over peach-milk mixture; let stand 1 minute. Stir in cinnamon and margarine or butter, if desired. Simmer over medium-low heat about 3 or 4 minutes, stirring frequently. Remove from heat; stir in vanilla. Cool peach mixture. Set aside 3/4 cup peach mixture in refrigerator. Stir 1/2 cup milk and yogurt into remaining peach mixture. Freeze in ice-cream maker according to manufacturer's directions. When frozen fold in chilled 3/4 cup peach mixture and vanilla wafers just enough to create a swirled effect. Or follow refrigerator-freezer instructions on page 4 or 5, and fold in chilled 3/4 cup peach mixture and vanilla wafers after final processing or beating just enough to create a swirled effect. Makes about 1 quart.

1 serving contains:

Cal	Prot	Carb	Fib	Fat	Chol	Sodium
133	4g	30g	1g	0	2mg	45mg

Toasted Almond Nectarine Frozen Yogurt

Toasted almonds join forces with nectarines to enhance the taste and texture.

1/4 cup toasted slivered almonds

1/2 cup sugar

1/4 teaspoon ground nutmeg

1/4 cup lowfat milk

1 teaspoon unflavored gelatin

4 ripe medium nectarines, seeded and quartered

1/4 cup light corn syrup

1 cup plain lowfat yogurt, stirred

In blender or food processor fitted with metal blade, combine toasted almonds, sugar and nutmeg. Process until nuts are finely chopped; set aside in medium bowl. In small saucepan, combine milk and gelatin; let stand 1 minute. Cook and stir over low heat until gelatin dissolves; set aside. Purée nectarines and corn syrup in blender or food processor; combine with almond mixture and dissolved gelatin. Stir in yogurt. Freeze in ice-cream maker according to manufacturer's directions; or follow refrigerator-freezer instructions on page 4. Makes about 1 quart.

1 serving contains:

Cal	Prot	Carb	Fib	Fat	Chol	Sodium
161	4g	31g	2g	3g	2mg	30mg

Sugar-Free Nectarine Frozen Yogurt

Fresh-fruit frozen yogurt without any sugar.

1/4 cup water

1 teaspoon unflavored gelatin

3 small ripe nectarines, seeded and quartered

12 (1-gram) packets Equal®

1 cup plain lowfat yogurt, stirred

1 egg white

1/3 cup cold water

1/3 cup nonfat dry milk

In small saucepan, combine 1/4 cup water and gelatin; let stand 1 minute. Cook and stir over low heat until gelatin dissolves; set aside. In blender or food processor fitted with metal blade, finely chop nectarines. Combine with Equal, yogurt and dissolved gelatin. In small bowl, combine egg white with 1/3 cup cold water and nonfat dry milk. Beat until stiff but not dry. Fold into nectarine mixture. Freeze in ice-cream maker according to manufacturer's directions; or follow refrigerator-freezer instructions on page 4. Makes about 1 quart.

1 serving contains:

Cal	Prot	Carb	Fib	Fat	Chol	Sodium
59	4g	10g	1g	1g	2mg	43mg

Orchard-Fresh Plum Frozen Yogurt

Plums that are ripe and slightly soft to the touch make the best frozen yogurt.

2/3 cup sugar

1 teaspoon cornstarch

1/2 cup lowfat milk

5 fresh plums, peeled and quartered

3 tablespoons light corn syrup

1 cup plain lowfat yogurt, stirred

In medium saucepan, combine sugar and cornstarch. Stir in milk. Cook and stir over moderate heat until bubbly; then cook 1 minute longer. Remove from heat. Combine plums and corn syrup in blender or food processor fitted with metal blade. Process until finely chopped. Add to cooked mixture; cool. Stir in yogurt. Freeze in ice-cream maker according to manufacturer's directions; or follow refrigerator-freezer instructions on page 4. Makes about 1 quart.

1 serving contains:

Cal	Prot	Carb	Fib	Fat	Chol	Sodium
119	2g	27g	1g	1g	2mg	29mg

Spicy Plum Frozen Yogurt

To make a spice bag, cut a 6-inch square of cheesecloth. Place whole spices in center; pull up sides and corners until they meet in center. Tie with string.

1 (3-inch) stick cinnamon, halved crosswise

6 whole cloves

6 whole allspice

1/2 cup unsweetened white grape juice

1/4 cup water

1 teaspoon unflavored gelatin

4 medium plums, seeded and quartered

1/2 cup sugar

1 cup plain lowfat yogurt, stirred

Tie cinnamon, cloves and allspice in cheesecloth. In medium sauce-pan, combine spice bag with grape juice. Simmer, covered, 5 minutes. Combine water and gelatin; let stand 1 minute to soften. Remove and discard spice bag from hot grape juice; immediately stir in softened gelatin. In blender or food processor fitted with metal blade, combine plums and sugar; process until plums are finely chopped. Add to grape-juice mixture; cool. Stir in yogurt. Freeze in ice-cream maker according to manufacturer's directions; or follow refrigerator-freezer instructions on page 4. Makes about 1 quart.

1 serving contains:

Cal	Prot	Carb	Fib	Fat	Chol	Sodium
98	3g	21g	1g	1g	2mg	22mg

Bit O' Gold Plum Frozen Yogurt

An occasional shred of orange peel makes an appetizing contrast to the red or purple flecks of plum.

1/2 cup orange juice

1 teaspoon unflavored gelatin

2/3 cup sugar

2 tablespoons light corn syrup

4 fresh plums, seeded and quartered

1/2 teaspoon vanilla extract

1/4 teaspoon grated orange peel

1 cup plain lowfat yogurt, stirred

In small saucepan, combine orange juice and gelatin; let stand one minute. Add sugar and corn syrup. Stir over low heat until gelatin dissolves; remove from heat. Finely chop plums in blender or food processor fitted with metal blade. Combine with gelatin mixture, vanilla and grated orange peel. Stir in yogurt. Freeze in ice-cream maker according to manufacturer's directions; or follow refrigerator-freezer instructions on page 4. Makes about 1 quart.

1 serving contains:

Cal	Prot	Carb	Fib	Fat	Chol	Sodium
126	3g	28g	1g	1g	2mg	24mg

Nutty Plum Frozen Yogurt

For your plum nutty yogurt-loving friends.

1/2 cup toasted pecans

1/2 cup sugar

1/4 teaspoon ground nutmeg

1/4 teaspoon ground ginger

2 strips orange peel, about 1/2 x 1 inch each*

3 plums, seeded and quartered

1/4 cup light corn syrup

1/4 cup cold water

1 teaspoon unflavored gelatin

1 cup plain lowfat yogurt, stirred

* Cut off and discard any white part of the orange peel before chopping it with other ingredients.

Combine pecans, sugar, nutmeg, ginger and orange peel in blender or food processor fitted with metal blade. Process until finely chopped. Pour into medium bowl. Process plums and corn syrup until finely chopped. In small saucepan, combine cold water and gelatin; let stand one minute. Cook and stir over low heat until dissolved. Add puréed plums and dissolved gelatin to pecan mixture. Stir in yogurt. Freeze in ice-cream maker according to manufacturer's directions; or follow refrigerator-freezer instructions on page 4. Makes about 1 quart.

1 serving contains:

Cal	Prot	Carb	Fib	Fat	Chol	Sodium
162	3g	27g	1g	5g	2mg	26mg

Burgundy Plum Frozen Yogurt

A refreshing treat that's especially welcome on a hot sultry day.

4 fresh plums, seeded and quartered

3/4 cup sugar

1/3 cup Burgundy wine

1/8 teaspoon ground cinnamon

1 teaspoon lemon juice

1/2 cup plain lowfat yogurt, stirred

In a blender or food processor fitted with metal blade, combine plums and sugar. Process until finely chopped. Add to Burgundy, cinnamon, lemon juice and yogurt. Freeze in ice-cream maker according to manufacturer's directions; or follow refrigerator-freezer instructions on page 4. Makes about 1 quart.

1 serving contains:

Cal	Prot	Carb	Fib	Fat	Chol	Sodium
106	1g	24g	1g	0	1mg	11mg

Fresh Apricot Frozen Yogurt

Take advantage of the short season for fresh apricots; use fully ripe ones for the best fresh-fruit flavor.

3 large ripe fresh apricots, pitted and coarsely chopped (about 10 oz.)

1/2 cup sugar

1/4 cup light corn syrup

1 tablespoon lemon juice

1/8 teaspoon almond extract

3/4 cup lowfat milk

1 cup plain lowfat yogurt, stirred

In blender or food processor fitted with metal blade, combine apricots, sugar, corn syrup, lemon juice and almond extract. Process until finely chopped. Stir in milk and yogurt. Freeze in ice-cream maker according to manufacturer's directions; or follow refrigerator-freezer instructions on page 4. Makes about 1 quart.

1 serving contains:

Cal	Prot	Carb	Fib	Fat	Chol	Sodium
121	3g	27g	1g	1g	3mg	37mg

Anytime Apricot Honey Frozen Yogurt

Keep a can of apricots on hand so you can whip up this frozen treat any day of the year.

1 (16- or 17-oz.) can unpeeled apricot halves in heavy syrup

1/3 cup sugar

2 teaspoons cornstarch

2 tablespoons honey

1-1/2 cups plain lowfat yogurt, stirred

1 tablespoon Amaretto® almond-flavored liqueur

In blender or food processor fitted with metal blade, purée apricots and their syrup; set aside. In medium saucepan, combine sugar and cornstarch. Stir in honey and puréed apricots. Cook and stir over medium heat until slightly thickened. Remove from heat; cool to lukewarm. Add yogurt and Amaretto. Freeze in ice-cream maker according to manufacturer's directions; or follow refrigerator-freezer instructions on page 4. Makes about 1 quart.

1 serving contains:

Cal	Prot	Carb	Fib	Fat	Chol	Sodium
124	3g	28g	1g	1g	3mg	33mg

Cherry-Berry Frozen Yogurt

Sweet dark cherries blend beautifully with cranberry juice; bright-red pie cherries are too tart.

1 cup cranberry juice cocktail

1 teaspoon unflavored gelatin

**1 cup fresh or frozen pitted
    sweet cherries**

2/3 cup sugar

**1 cup plain lowfat yogurt,
    stirred**

In small pan, combine cranberry juice and gelatin; let stand 1 minute. Cook and stir over low heat until gelatin dissolves. In blender or food processor fitted with metal blade, combine pitted cherries and sugar; process until almost smooth. Combine with dissolved gelatin. Stir in yogurt. Freeze in ice-cream maker according to manufacturer's directions; or follow refrigerator-freezer instructions on page 4. Makes about 1 quart.

1 serving contains:

Cal	Prot	Carb	Fib	Fat	Chol	Sodium
118	3g	26g	1g	1g	2mg	22mg

Port 'O Pear Frozen Yogurt

Port wine is a flattering flavor for fresh pears and yogurt.

3 ripe pears, peeled, cored and cubed

1/2 cup port wine

1/4 teaspoon grated lemon peel

1 stick cinnamon

1/2 cup sugar

2 teaspoons cornstarch

1/4 cup lowfat milk

1 cup plain lowfat yogurt, stirred

In medium saucepan, combine pears, wine, lemon peel, cinnamon and sugar. Cover and simmer about 3 minutes or until pears are almost soft; remove from heat. Dissolve cornstarch in milk. Stir into hot pear mixture. Return to heat and simmer another 3 or 4 minutes or until pears are soft. Discard cinnamon stick. Pour mixture into blender or food processor fitted with metal blade. Process until finely chopped; cool. Stir in yogurt. Freeze in ice-cream maker according to manufacturer's directions; or follow refrigerator-freezer instructions on page 4. Makes about 1 quart.

1 serving contains:

Cal	Prot	Carb	Fib	Fat	Chol	Sodium
119	2g	25g	2g	1g	2mg	25mg

A Taste of Autumn

Savor the bounty of fall with this creamy blend of grapes and pears.

1/2 cup lowfat milk

1 teaspoon unflavored gelatin

2 small or 1 large pear, peeled, seeded and quartered

1 teaspoon lemon juice

1/2 cup Concord grape juice

1/2 cup sugar

1/4 cup light corn syrup

1 cup lowfat yogurt, stirred

In small saucepan, combine milk and gelatin; let stand 1 minute. Cook and stir over low heat until gelatin dissolves; set aside. In blender or food processor fitted with metal blade, combine pears, lemon juice, grape juice, sugar and corn syrup. Process until pears are chopped; stir in dissolved gelatin and yogurt. Freeze in ice-cream maker according to manufacturer's directions; or follow refrigerator-freezer instructions on page 4. Makes about 1 quart.

1 serving contains:

Cal	Prot	Carb	Fib	Fat	Chol	Sodium
127	3g	28g	1g	1g	2mg	34mg

Red-Hot Apple Frozen Yogurt

To shorten the preparation time on this popular flavor combination, substitute 1 cup unsweetened applesauce for the 2 tart apples and lemon juice.

2 small tart apples, peeled, cored and cut into wedges

1-1/2 teaspoons lemon juice

1/2 cup sugar

1 teaspoon cornstarch

1 cup lowfat milk

1/2 cup red-hot cinnamon candies

1 cup plain lowfat yogurt, stirred

In blender or food processor fitted with metal blade, combine apple wedges and lemon juice. Process until puréed; set aside. In medium saucepan, combine sugar and cornstarch. Stir in milk and cinnamon candies. Cook and stir over medium-low heat until mixture simmers. Cook and stir 1 minute longer or until cinnamon candies are dissolved. Remove from heat; stir in puréed apples. Cool; stir in yogurt. Freeze in ice-cream maker according to manufacturer's directions; or follow refrigerator-freezer instructions on page 4. Makes about 1 quart.

1 serving contains:

Cal	Prot	Carb	Fib	Fat	Chol	Sodium
153	3g	35g	1g	1g	3mg	39mg

Maple Apple Frozen Yogurt

The slightly offbeat flavor combination of maple syrup with apple is reminiscent of favorite foods from childhood days.

1 cooking apple, peeled, cored and finely chopped

1 cup maple-flavored syrup

1/8 teaspoon ground cardamom

2 teaspoons unflavored gelatin

1/2 cup lowfat milk

1 cup plain lowfat yogurt, stirred

In medium saucepan, combine apple, maple-flavored syrup and cardamom. Cover and simmer until apple pieces are very soft. In the meantime, sprinkle gelatin over milk; let stand 1 minute. Add to hot apple mixture. Stir until gelatin is dissolved. Cool; add yogurt. Freeze in ice-cream maker according to manufacturer's directions; or follow refrigerator-freezer instructions on page 4. Makes about 1 quart.

1 serving contains:

Cal	Prot	Carb	Fib	Fat	Chol	Sodium
149	4g	32g	1g	1g	2mg	36mg

Citrus Fruits

Golden Glow Frozen Yogurt

Gingered Orange Refresher

Orange-Cranberry-Pecan Frozen Yogurt

Candied Orange Honey Crunch

Lemon Cheese Frozen Yogurt

Sugar-Free Tangerine Frozen Yogurt

Tangerine Pistachio Swirl

Key Lime Frozen Yogurt

Golden Glow Frozen Yogurt

Refreshing fresh orange flavor makes a mouth-watering finale to a special dinner.

1 orange

2/3 cup sugar

1 teaspoon unflavored gelatin

1-1/2 cups orange juice

2 tablespoons honey

1-1/2 cups plain lowfat yogurt, stirred

With zester or paring knife, cut peel from orange, being careful not to include any of the white part. Combine peel with sugar in blender or food processor fitted with metal blade; process until finely minced. Set aside. In medium saucepan, combine gelatin and orange juice; let stand one minute. Stir over low heat until gelatin dissolves. Add honey. Combine with processed orange peel. Strain; discard peel. Cool. Stir in yogurt. Freeze in ice-cream maker according to manufacturer's directions; or follow refrigerator-freezer instructions on page 4. Makes about 1 quart.

1 serving contains:

Cal	Prot	Carb	Fib	Fat	Chol	Sodium
140	4g	31g	1g	1g	3mg	32mg

Gingered Orange Refresher

Because orange juice is the predominant ingredient in this dessert, the result is a very refreshing treat.

1-1/2 cups orange juice

12 (1/8-inch-thick) crosswise slices fresh ginger (about 1 oz.)

1/4 teaspoon grated orange peel

1/3 cup sugar

1 cup miniature marshmallows or cut-up large marshmallows

3/4 cup lowfat milk

1 cup plain lowfat yogurt, stirred

In 1- or 1-1/2-quart saucepan combine orange juice, ginger, orange peel, sugar and marshmallows. Cook over very low heat, stirring frequently about 15 minutes or until marshmallows dissolve. Remove and discard ginger slices. Cool orange mixture; then stir in milk and yogurt until well blended. Freeze in ice-cream maker according to manufacturer's directions; or follow refrigerator-freezer instructions on page 4. Makes about 1 quart.

1 serving contains:

Cal	Prot	Carb	Fib	Fat	Chol	Sodium
105	3g	23g	0	1g	3mg	39mg

Orange Cranberry-Pecan Frozen Yogurt

A beautiful dessert to enhance holiday entertaining.

1 large orange, peeled, seeded and cut into chunks

1 cup fresh cranberries

3/4 cup sugar

2 tablespoons light corn syrup

1 teaspoon unflavored gelatin

3/4 cup lowfat milk

1 cup plain lowfat yogurt, stirred

1/4 cup finely chopped pecans or walnuts*

*If this recipe will be frozen in a refrigerator freezer, see page 4 or 5 before adding this ingredient.

In blender or food processor fitted with metal blade, finely chop orange. Add cranberries, sugar and corn syrup. Process until cranberries are finely chopped. In small saucepan, combine gelatin and milk; let stand about 1 minute. Stir over low heat until gelatin dissolves. Combine with puréed cranberry mixture. Stir in yogurt and nuts. Freeze in ice-cream maker according to manufacturer's directions; or follow refrigerator-freezer instructions on page 4. Makes about 1 quart.

1 serving contains:

Cal	Prot	Carb	Fib	Fat	Chol	Sodium
157	4g	30g	1g	3g	3mg	36mg

Candied Orange Honey Crunch

Muesli ingredients vary with the manufacturer—it's usually a combination of cereal, dried fruits and nuts.

1 medium orange

1/2 cup sugar

1/2 cup water

1 teaspoon chopped crystallized ginger

1 (1.3-oz.) envelope Dream Whip® whipped topping mix

3 tablespoons honey

1-1/2 cups plain lowfat yogurt, stirred

1/4 cup Muesli

Remove orange peel in small strips. Be careful to include only the orange-colored part of the peel, not any of the white part. Squeeze juice from the orange, set aside. In small saucepan, combine peel, sugar and water. Bring to boil, simmer about 20 to 30 minutes or until peel is soft and syrup thickens, cool. In blender or food processor fitted with metal blade, process cooled orange syrup (with peel), ginger and reserved orange juice until peel is finely chopped; combine with topping mix and honey in medium bowl. Stir in yogurt. Freeze in ice-cream maker according to manufacturer's directions. When frozen, stir in Muesli. Or follow refrigerator-freezer instructions on page 4 and stir in Muesli after final processing or beating. Makes about 1 quart.

1 serving contains:

Cal	Prot	Carb	Fib	Fat	Chol	Sodium
149	3g	29g	1g	3g	3mg	43mg

Lemon Cheese Frozen Yogurt

A first cousin of the ever-popular lemon cheesecake.

1/4 cup lowfat milk

1 teaspoon unflavored gelatin

1 cup ricotta cheese

3/4 cup sugar

1/2 teaspoon grated lemon peel

1/4 cup lemon juice

1-1/2 cups plain lowfat yogurt, stirred

In small saucepan, combine milk and gelatin; let stand 1 minute. Stir over low heat until gelatin dissolves. Remove from heat; set aside. In blender or food processor fitted with metal blade, combine ricotta cheese, sugar and lemon peel. Process until ricotta is smooth. Stir in lemon juice, dissolved gelatin and yogurt. Freeze in ice-cream maker according to manufacturer's directions; or follow refrigerator-freezer instructions on page 4. Makes about 1 quart.

1 serving contains:

Cal	Prot	Carb	Fib	Fat	Chol	Sodium
151	7g	24g	0	3g	12mg	75mg

Sugar-Free Tangerine Frozen Yogurt

No one will believe you made this great frozen yogurt without any sugar.

1/4 cup water

1 teaspoon unflavored gelatin

1/2 teaspoon grated tangerine peel

1 cup tangerine juice (6 to 8 small tangerines)

12 (1-gram) packets Equal®

1 cup plain nonfat yogurt, stirred

1 egg white

1/3 cup water

1/3 cup nonfat dry milk

In small saucepan, combine water and gelatin; let stand 1 minute. Stir over low heat until gelatin dissolves. In medium bowl, combine dissolved gelatin, tangerine peel, juice and Equal. Stir in yogurt. Beat egg white with 1/3 cup water and dry milk until stiff but not dry. Fold into tangerine-yogurt mixture. Freeze in ice-cream maker according to manufacturer's directions; or follow refrigerator-freezer instructions on page 4. Makes about 1 quart.

1 serving contains:

Cal	Prot	Carb	Fib	Fat	Chol	Sodium
60	4g	11g	1g	0	1mg	45mg

Tangerine Pistachio Swirl

Natural pistachios are recommended as they blend best with the green food coloring in the pistachio swirl.

3/4 cup lowfat milk

2/3 cup miniature or cut-up large marshmallows

1/2 cup pistachios

4 or 5 drops green food coloring, optional

1 teaspoon unflavored gelatin

1/2 cup lowfat milk

1-1/2 cups tangerine juice

3/4 cup sugar

1/2 teaspoon vanilla extract

1 cup plain lowfat yogurt, stirred

In small saucepan, combine 3/4 cup milk and marshmallows. Cook and stir over low heat until marshmallows dissolve. Remove from heat; pour into blender or food processor fitted with metal blade. Add nuts and process until almost smooth. While processing, add food coloring (if desired) 1 drop at a time. Refrigerate. In small saucepan, sprinkle gelatin over 1/2 cup milk; let stand 1 minute. Then cook and stir over low heat just until gelatin dissolves. Remove from heat; cool. In medium bowl, combine cooled gelatin mixture, tangerine juice, sugar, vanilla and yogurt. Stir until sugar is dissolved. Freeze in ice-cream maker according to manufacturer's directions. When frozen, stir in pistachio-marshmallow mixture just enough to create a swirled effect. Or follow refrigerator-freezer instructions on page 4, and stir in pistachio-marshmallow mixture after final processing or beating. Makes about 1 quart.

1 serving contains:

Cal	Prot	Carb	Fib	Fat	Chol	Sodium
192	6g	33g	1g	5g	3mg	46mg

Key Lime Frozen Yogurt

What could be more appealing and timesaving than this tantalizing sweet-sour combination of three ingredients?

1 cup plain lowfat yogurt, stirred

1 (14-oz.) can sweetened condensed milk

1 (6-oz.) can frozen limeade concentrate, undiluted and partially thawed

In medium bowl, combine yogurt and condensed milk. Stir in undiluted and partially thawed limeade concentrate. Freeze in ice-cream maker according to manufacturer's directions; or follow refrigerator-freezer instructions on page 4. Makes about 1 quart.

1 serving contains:

Cal	Prot	Carb	Fib	Fat	Chol	Sodium
217	6g	39g	0	5g	19mg	83mg

Tropical Fruits

Classic Banana Frozen Yogurt

Banana Macadamia Special

Banana Orange Yogurt with Sweet 'n Low®

Taste of the Tropics

Fresh Piña Colada Frozen Yogurt

Shortcut Frozen Piña Colada

Coconut Pineapple Pudding Special

Coconut Custard Frozen Yogurt

Island Treat

Fruit Gazpacho Frozen Yogurt

Mango Yogurt Freeze

Tradewinds Frozen Yogurt

Mango Apricot Frozen Yogurt

Oasis Frozen Yogurt

Classic Banana Frozen Yogurt

A favorite banana frozen yogurt that appeals to all ages.

2 medium bananas, peeled and quartered

1/2 cup sugar

2 tablespoons honey

1 tablespoon lemon juice

1/2 cup lowfat milk

1 cup plain lowfat yogurt, stirred

In blender or food processor fitted with metal blade, combine bananas, sugar, honey and lemon juice. Process until bananas are puréed. Stir in milk and yogurt. Freeze in ice-cream maker according to manufacturer's directions; or follow refrigerator-freezer instructions on page 4. Makes about 1 quart.

1 serving contains:

Cal	Prot	Carb	Fib	Fat	Chol	Sodium
115	2g	26g	1g	1g	2mg	29mg

Banana Macadamia Special

So super that you'll think you're on an island plantation in Hawaii.

1/2 cup lowfat milk

1 teaspoon unflavored gelatin

2 medium bananas, peeled and quartered

2 tablespoons light corn syrup

1/2 cup sugar

1 teaspoon lemon juice

1/2 teaspoon vanilla extract

1 cup plain lowfat yogurt, stirred

1/4 cup chopped macadamia nuts*

In small saucepan, combine milk and gelatin; let stand one minute. Stir over low heat until gelatin dissolves; set aside. In blender or food processor fitted with metal blade, combine bananas, corn syrup, sugar, lemon juice and vanilla. Process until bananas are puréed. Combine with yogurt and macadamia nuts. Freeze in ice-cream maker according to manufacturer's directions; or follow refrigerator-freezer instructions on page 4 and stir in nuts after final processing or beating. Makes about 1 quart.

1 serving contains:

Cal	Prot	Carb	Fib	Fat	Chol	Sodium
147	4g	26g	1g	4g	2mg	32mg

*If this recipe will be frozen in a refrigerator freezer, see page 4 or 5 before adding this ingredient.

Banana Orange Yogurt with Sweet 'n Low®

Enjoy banana frozen yogurt with only half the usual sugar.

2 medium bananas, peeled and quartered

4 (1 gram) packets Sweet 'n Low® sweetener

1/3 cup sugar

2/3 cup orange juice

1 cup plain lowfat yogurt, stirred

In blender or food processor fitted with metal blade, purée bananas with sweetener, sugar and orange juice. Stir in yogurt. Freeze in ice-cream maker according to manufacturer's directions; or follow refrigerator-freezer instructions on page 4. Makes about 1 quart.

1 serving contains:

Cal	Prot	Carb	Fib	Fat	Chol	Sodium
85	2g	19g	1g	1g	2mg	21mg

Taste of the Tropics

Take advantage of tropical fruits that are available in your market; create an exciting exotic dessert.

1 (8-oz.) can crushed pineapple in unsweetened juice

1 teaspoon unflavored gelatin

1 small papaya, peeled, seeded and cut into chunks

1 small banana, peeled and cut into chunks

1/2 cup sugar

2 tablespoons honey

1 cup plain lowfat yogurt, stirred

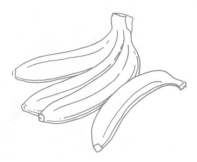

In small saucepan, combine pineapple and gelatin; let stand one minute. Cook and stir over low heat until gelatin dissolves; set aside. In blender or food processor fitted with metal blade, combine papaya, banana, sugar and honey. Process until fruit is finely chopped. Combine with pineapple mixture. Stir in yogurt. Freeze in ice-cream maker according to manufacturer's directions; or follow refrigerator-freezer instructions on page 4. Makes about 1 quart.

1 serving contains:

Cal	Prot	Carb	Fib	Fat	Chol	Sodium
131	3g	30g	1g	1g	2mg	23mg

Fresh Piña Colada Frozen Yogurt

Reminiscent of exotic fresh-fruit concoctions from the Caribbean.

1 banana, peeled and quartered

2 cups ripe fresh pineapple chunks

1/4 cup flaked coconut

1/2 cup brown sugar

2 tablespoons rum or rum flavoring

1 cup vanilla lowfat yogurt, stirred

In blender or food processor fitted with metal blade, combine banana, pineapple and coconut. Blend until almost smooth. Add brown sugar and rum or rum flavoring. Stir in yogurt. Freeze in ice-cream maker according to manufacturer's directions; or follow refrigerator-freezer instructions on page 4. Makes about 1 quart.

1 serving contains:

Cal	Prot	Carb	Fib	Fat	Chol	Sodium
120	2g	24g	1g	1g	2mg	27mg

Shortcut Frozen Piña Colada

For all those with a sweet tooth. It's quite smooth and rich tasting, slightly sweeter than most frozen yogurts.

1 (8-oz.) can crushed pineapple in unsweetened juice

1 (16-oz.) can cream of coconut

1 tablespoon rum or rum flavoring

1 cup plain lowfat yogurt, stirred

In medium bowl, combine pineapple with juice, cream of coconut, rum or rum flavoring and plain lowfat yogurt. Freeze in ice-cream maker according to manufacturer's directions; or follow refrigerator-freezer instructions on page 4. Makes about 1 quart.

1 serving contains:

Cal	Prot	Carb	Fib	Fat	Chol	Sodium
151	3g	8g	1g	13g	2mg	28mg

Coconut Pineapple Pudding Special

You don't have to add sugar when you start with a base of sugar-free instant pudding.

3/4 cup lowfat milk

1 cup plain lowfat yogurt, stirred

1 (0.9-oz.) package sugar-free instant vanilla pudding

1 (8-1/2-oz.) can crushed pineapple in unsweetened pineapple juice

1/4 cup flaked coconut

In medium bowl, combine milk, yogurt and sugar-free instant vanilla pudding. Whisk about one minute or until mixture is smooth. Stir undrained pineapple and coconut into pudding mixture. Freeze in ice-cream maker according to manufacturer's directions; or follow refrigerator-freezer instructions on page 4. Makes about 1 quart.

1 serving contains:

Cal	Prot	Carb	Fib	Fat	Chol	Sodium
58	3g	9g	1g	1g	3mg	36mg

Coconut Custard Frozen Yogurt

Ingredients borrowed from old-fashioned coconut pie. Blend with vanilla yogurt for a timely new dessert.

1 cup flaked coconut

1 cup lowfat milk

1 egg, slightly beaten

1/2 cup sugar

1/2 teaspoon vanilla extract

2 cups vanilla lowfat yogurt, stirred

In blender or food processor fitted with metal blade, combine coconut and milk. Process until coconut is finely chopped. In small saucepan, combine with beaten egg and sugar. Cook and stir over moderate heat until thickened. Strain; discard pieces of coconut. Stir in vanilla and yogurt. Freeze in ice-cream maker according to manufacturer's directions; or follow refrigerator-freezer instructions on page 4. Makes about 1 quart.

1 serving contains:

Cal	Prot	Carb	Fib	Fat	Chol	Sodium
161	5g	26g	1g	5g	31mg	63mg

Island Treat

Papaya combined with lime juice—a more refreshing, mouth-watering frozen dessert would be hard to come by.

1/2 cup lowfat milk

1 teaspoon unflavored gelatin

1 large ripe papaya, peeled, seeded and cubed (about 1 lb.)

1/2 cup sugar

2 tablespoons honey

1 tablespoon lime juice

1-1/2 cups plain lowfat yogurt, stirred

In small saucepan, combine milk and gelatin; let stand 1 minute. Stir over low heat until gelatin dissolves; set aside. In blender or food processor fitted with metal blade, purée papaya, sugar, honey and lime juice until almost smooth. Combine papaya purée, gelatin mixture and yogurt. Freeze in ice-cream maker according to manufacturer's directions; or follow refrigerator-freezer instructions on page 4. Makes about 1 quart.

1 serving contains:

Cal	Prot	Carb	Fib	Fat	Chol	Sodium
124	4g	26g	1g	1g	3mg	41mg

Fruit Gazpacho Frozen Yogurt

An unusual combination of flavors for a delicious change-of-pace yogurt.

1/2 cup lowfat milk

2 slices raisin or cinnamon bread, quartered

1/2 teaspoon ground cardamom

1/2 cup sugar

1/2 teaspoon grated orange peel

1 cup chopped and seeded cantaloupe or crenshaw melon

1 small papaya, peeled, seeded and chopped

1/2 cup toasted slivered almonds

3/4 cup plain lowfat yogurt

In food processor fitted with metal blade, combine milk, bread, cardamom, sugar and orange peel; process briefly. Add chopped cantaloupe or crenshaw melon, papaya and toasted almonds. Process until fruit is finely chopped but not puréed. Stir in yogurt. Freeze in ice-cream maker according to manufacturer's directions; or follow refrigerator-freezer instructions on page 4. Makes about 1 quart.

1 serving contains:

Cal	Prot	Carb	Fib	Fat	Chol	Sodium
157	4g	25g	2g	5g	2mg	50mg

Mango Yogurt Freeze

Cut mango into cubes before puréeing to avoid the slightly stringy texture often associated with this fruit.

1/2 cup sugar

1 tablespoon cornstarch

1/2 cup orange juice

1/2 teaspoon grated orange peel

1/2 cup lowfat milk

2 tablespoons light corn syrup

1 large mango, peeled and cubed

1 tablespoon Amaretto® almond-flavored liqueur

3/4 cup plain lowfat yogurt, stirred

In small saucepan, combine sugar and cornstarch. Stir in orange juice, peel, milk and corn syrup. Cook and stir over moderate heat until mixture simmers. Cook 2 minutes longer or until translucent and slightly thickened. Remove from heat. In blender or food processor fitted with metal blade, purée mango with Amaretto. Add to cooked mixture; cool. Stir in yogurt. Freeze in ice-cream maker according to manufacturer's directions; or follow refrigerator-freezer instructions on page 4. Makes about 1 quart.

1 serving contains:

Cal	Prot	Carb	Fib	Fat	Chol	Sodium
110	2g	26g	1g	1g	2mg	26mg

Tradewinds Frozen Yogurt

For maximum mango flavor, choose fruit that gives easily when lightly pressed with fingers.

1/2 cup pineapple juice

1 teaspoon unflavored gelatin

1 medium mango, peeled and cubed

1/2 cup sugar

3 tablespoons honey

3/4 cup milk

1/4 teaspoon vanilla extract

3/4 cup plain lowfat yogurt, stirred

In small saucepan, combine pineapple juice and gelatin; let stand one minute. Cook and stir over low heat until gelatin dissolves; set aside. In blender or food processor fitted with metal blade, combine mango cubes and sugar. Purée until smooth. Combine with honey, milk, vanilla and dissolved gelatin. Stir in yogurt. Freeze in ice-cream maker according to manufacturer's directions; or follow refrigerator-freezer instructions on page 4. Makes about 1 quart.

1 serving contains:

Cal	Prot	Carb	Fib	Fat	Chol	Sodium
125	3g	28g	1g	1g	2mg	29mg

Mango Apricot Frozen Yogurt

Mango pulp clings to a large seed in the center of the fruit. Slice strips of pulp away from the seed; then cut pulp crosswise into small cubes.

2 medium mangoes, peeled and cubed

1/2 cup apricot-pineapple juice

1/3 cup sugar

1/8 teaspoon ground mace

3/4 cup plain lowfat yogurt, stirred

In blender or food processor fitted with metal blade, combine mangoes, apricot-pineapple juice and sugar. Purée until smooth. Stir in ground mace and yogurt. Freeze in ice-cream maker according to manufacturer's directions; or follow refrigerator-freezer instructions on page 4. Makes about 1 quart.

1 serving contains:

Cal	Prot	Carb	Fib	Fat	Chol	Sodium
88	1g	21g	2g	0	1mg	16mg

Oasis Frozen Yogurt

Dates provide a welcome contrast to slightly tart orange yogurt.

2 teaspoons cornstarch

1/4 cup sugar

1 cup milk

2 tablespoons honey

1/2 teaspoon grated orange peel

3/4 cup finely chopped dates

2 cups lowfat orange yogurt, stirred

In medium saucepan, combine cornstarch and sugar; stir in milk, honey and orange peel. Cook and stir over moderate heat until translucent (about 5 minutes). Remove from heat. Add dates; cool. Stir in yogurt. Freeze in ice-cream maker according to manufacturer's directions; or follow refrigerator-freezer instructions on page 4. Makes about 1 quart.

1 serving contains:

Cal	Prot	Carb	Fib	Fat	Chol	Sodium
159	4g	36g	1g	1g	4mg	48mg

Exotic Fruits

Passion Fruit Frozen Yogurt

Persimmon Frozen Yogurt

Fresh Pomegranate Frozen Yogurt

Kiwi Lime Frozen Yogurt

Sunshine Kiwi Freeze

Honey Ginger Feijoa Frozen Yogurt

Strawberry Feijoa Refresher

Sunshine Medley Frozen Yogurt

Spicy Pumpkin Favorite

Harvest Moon Frozen Yogurt

Passion Fruit Frozen Yogurt

Ready-to-eat fresh passion fruit is a strange-looking withered egg-shape tropical fruit from New Zealand with a wonderful tartly sweet flavor.

1/2 cup lowfat milk

1 teaspoon unflavored gelatin

5 passion fruit

3/4 cup sugar

1 teaspoon lemon juice

1-1/2 cups plain lowfat yogurt, stirred

1 egg white

1/3 cup water

1/3 cup nonfat dry milk

In small saucepan, combine milk and gelatin; let stand 1 minute. Cook and stir over low heat until gelatin dissolves; set aside. Cut each passion fruit in half crosswise; scoop out pulp and seeds. Discard shell. In blender or food processor fitted with metal blade, purée pulp and seeds. Strain; discard seeds. Combine passion fruit juice with sugar, lemon juice and dissolved gelatin. Stir in yogurt. In medium bowl, combine egg white, water and nonfat dry milk. Beat until stiff but not dry. Fold into yogurt mixture. Freeze in ice-cream maker according to manufacturer's directions; or follow refrigerator-freezer instructions on page 4. Makes about 1 quart.

1 serving contains:

Cal	Prot	Carb	Fib	Fat	Chol	Sodium
133	5g	27g	2g	1g	4mg	64mg

Persimmon Frozen Yogurt

Hachiya, a fig-shape persimmon, has a bright golden-orange color and should not be used until it is very soft. The tomato-shape Fuyu is reddish-orange and may be used when soft but slightly firm.

2 large or 3 small ripe persimmons, peeled and seeded

1 teaspoon lemon juice

1/2 cup sugar

2 tablespoons light corn syrup

1 teaspoon unflavored gelatin

1/4 cup lowfat milk

1 cup plain lowfat yogurt, stirred

In blender or food processor fitted with metal blade, purée persimmons with lemon juice, sugar and corn syrup. In small saucepan, sprinkle gelatin over milk; let stand 1 minute. Cook and stir over low heat until gelatin dissolves. Combine with persimmon purée. Stir in yogurt. Freeze in ice-cream maker according to manufacturer's directions; or follow refrigerator-freezer instructions on page 4. Makes about 1 quart.

1 serving contains:

Cal	Prot	Carb	Fib	Fat	Chol	Sodium
117	3g	27g	1g	1g	2mg	28mg

Fresh Pomegranate Frozen Yogurt

Fresh bright-red pomegranates are filled with many seeds coated with very juicy crimson pulp.

2 whole fresh pomegranates (8 to 10 oz. each)

1 cup lowfat milk

1 teaspoon unflavored gelatin

1/4 cup sugar

1/3 cup corn syrup

1 cup lowfat yogurt, stirred

Halve pomegranate crosswise. Remove juice with a citrus juicer; strain and discard seeds. In medium saucepan, combine milk and gelatin; let stand 1 minute. Stir in sugar and corn syrup. Cook and stir over low heat until gelatin dissolves. Remove from heat; cool. Add yogurt and pomegranate juice. Freeze in ice-cream maker according to manufacturer's directions; or follow refrigerator-freezer instructions on page 4. Makes about 1 quart.

1 serving contains:

Cal	Prot	Carb	Fib	Fat	Chol	Sodium
135	4g	30g	1g	1g	3mg	44mg

Kiwi Lime Frozen Yogurt

Unripe kiwi has very little flavor.
Be sure fruit is ripe.

**2 ripe kiwi, peeled and
quartered**

4 teaspoons lime juice

3/4 cup sugar

1/2 teaspoon vanilla extract

1 cup lowfat milk

**1 cup plain lowfat yogurt,
stirred**

**3 or 4 drops green food
coloring**

1/4 cup chopped pistachios*

In blender or food processor
fitted with metal blade, combine
kiwi, lime juice, sugar and vanilla.
Process until almost smooth. In
medium bowl, combine puréed
mixture, milk, yogurt, food
coloring and pistachios. Stir until
well blended. Freeze in ice-cream
maker according to manufacturer's directions; or follow
refrigerator-freezer instructions
on page 4. Makes about 1 quart.

1 serving contains:

Cal	Prot	Carb	Fib	Fat	Chol	Sodium
138	4g	26g	1g	3g	3mg	37mg

*If this recipe will be frozen in a
  refrigerator freezer, see page 4
  or 5 before adding this
  ingredient.

Sunshine Kiwi Freeze

This refreshing combination of flavors makes an ideal dessert for entertaining.

3/4 cup sugar

1 egg

1 cup lowfat milk

2 ripe kiwi, peeled

1/3 cup orange juice

1/4 teaspoon vanilla extract

3 or 4 drops green food coloring, optional

1 cup plain lowfat yogurt

In small saucepan, combine sugar and egg; beat until well blended. Add milk; cook, stirring frequently, over medium-low heat 10 to 15 minutes or until mixture thickens and coats a metal spoon. Remove from heat; cool. In blender or food processor, purée kiwi with orange juice. Add puréed kiwi, vanilla, food coloring (if desired) and yogurt to cooled egg mixture. Freeze in ice-cream maker according to manufacturer's directions; or follow refrigerator-freezer instructions on page 4. Makes about 1 quart.

1 serving contains:

Cal	Prot	Carb	Fib	Fat	Chol	Sodium
128	4g	26g	1g	1g	30mg	44mg

Honey Ginger Feijoa Frozen Yogurt

Feijoas are sweet, aromatic, egg-shape grey-green tropical fruits. They are also known as guavas.

5 feijoas (guavas)

1 teaspoon lemon juice

1/2 teaspoon grated fresh ginger

1/2 cup sugar

2 teaspoons cornstarch

1-1/4 cups lowfat milk

1/4 cup honey

1 cup plain lowfat yogurt, stirred

Halve feijoas; scoop out pulp and discard shell. In blender or food processor fitted with metal blade, purée feijoa pulp, lemon juice and grated ginger. In medium saucepan, combine sugar and cornstarch; stir in milk and honey. Cook and stir until mixture simmers. Cook 1 minute longer; remove from heat. Add puréed feijoas. Stir in yogurt. Freeze in ice-cream maker according to manufacturer's directions; or follow refrigerator-freezer instructions on page 4. Makes about 1 quart.

1 serving contains:

Cal	Prot	Carb	Fib	Fat	Chol	Sodium
145	3g	32g	3g	1g	3mg	41mg

Strawberry Feijoa Refresher

Feijoas with the consistency of ripe tomatoes have just the right texture to use in a recipe.

2 large feijoas (guavas)

1 cup fresh or frozen unsweetened strawberries

1/2 cup sugar

1/2 cup lowfat milk

1 teaspoon unflavored gelatin

1/4 cup light corn syrup

1 cup plain lowfat yogurt, stirred

Halve feijoas; scoop out pulp and discard shell. In blender or food processor fitted with metal blade, purée pulp and strawberries with sugar. In small saucepan, combine milk and gelatin; let stand 1 minute. Cook and stir over low heat until gelatin dissolves. Combine with corn syrup and fruit. Stir in yogurt. Freeze in ice-cream maker according to manufacturer's directions; or follow refrigerator-freezer instructions on page 4. Makes about 1 quart.

1 serving contains:

Cal	Prot	Carb	Fib	Fat	Chol	Sodium
122	3g	27g	2g	1g	2mg	34mg

Sunshine Medley Frozen Yogurt

A refreshing tropical-fruit combination that will add a mouth-watering finale to any meal.

2 teaspoons cornstarch

2/3 cup sugar

3/4 cup pineapple juice

4 feijoas (guavas)

1 teaspoon lime juice

3/4 cup lowfat milk

1 cup plain lowfat yogurt, stirred

In medium saucepan, combine cornstarch and sugar; stir in pineapple juice. Cook and stir over moderate heat until mixture simmers. Cook one minute longer; remove from heat. Halve feijoas; scoop out pulp and discard shell. In blender or food processor fitted with metal blade, purée feijoa pulp and lime juice. Combine with pineapple mixture and milk. Stir in yogurt. Freeze in ice-cream maker according to manufacturer's directions; or follow refrigerator-freezer instructions on page 4. Makes about 1 quart.

1 serving contains:

Cal	Prot	Carb	Fib	Fat	Chol	Sodium
130	3g	29g	3g	1g	3mg	33mg

Spicy Pumpkin Favorite

All the wonderful aromas of Grandma's pumpkin pies.

1-1/4 cups lowfat milk

1/2 cup brown sugar

1 cup canned pumpkin

1 egg, slightly beaten

**1/2 teaspoon ground
cinnamon**

1/8 teaspoon ground nutmeg

1/8 teaspoon ground allspice

**1 cup plain lowfat yogurt,
stirred**

In medium saucepan, combine milk, brown sugar, pumpkin, egg, cinnamon, nutmeg and allspice. Cook and stir over low heat until slightly thickened. Cool; stir in yogurt. Freeze in ice-cream maker according to manufacturer's directions; or follow refrigerator-freezer instructions on page 4. Makes about 1 quart.

1 serving contains:

Cal	Prot	Carb	Fib	Fat	Chol	Sodium
106	4g	20g	1g	2g	29mg	55mg

Harvest Moon Frozen Yogurt

Frosty pumpkin dessert that's enhanced by orange juice and honey.

3/4 cup orange juice

1 teaspoon unflavored gelatin

1 cup canned pumpkin

1/3 cup brown sugar, lightly packed

1/4 cup honey

1/4 teaspoon ground cinnamon

1/8 teaspoon ground cloves

1/8 teaspoon ground ginger

1 cup plain lowfat yogurt, stirred

In medium saucepan, combine orange juice and gelatin; let stand 1 minute. Cook and stir over low heat until gelatin dissolves. Remove from heat. Then stir in pumpkin, brown sugar, honey, cinnamon, cloves and ginger; cool. Add yogurt. Freeze in ice-cream maker according to manufacturer's directions; or follow refrigerator-freezer instructions on page 4. Makes about 1 quart.

1 serving contains:

Cal	Prot	Carb	Fib	Fat	Chol	Sodium
109	3g	25g	1g	1g	2mg	27mg

Grapes & Melon

Concord Grape Frozen Yogurt

Grape 'n Lemon Frozen Yogurt

Watermelon Punch Frozen Yogurt

Honeydew Refresher

Honey Gingered Cantaloupe Frozen Yogurt

Concord Grape Frozen Yogurt

Take advantage of the short season that fresh Concord grapes are in the markets.

2 cups fresh Concord grapes

1/2 cup sugar

2 teaspoons cornstarch

1/4 cup light corn syrup

1 cup lowfat milk

1-1/4 cups plain lowfat yogurt, stirred

In blender or food processor fitted with metal blade, purée grapes. Strain and discard skins and seeds; set aside juice. In small saucepan, combine sugar and cornstarch; stir in corn syrup and milk. Cook and stir over low heat 6 to 8 minutes or until mixture simmers. Stir in strained grape juice and yogurt. Freeze in ice-cream maker according to manufacturer's directions; or follow refrigerator-freezer instructions on page 4. Makes about 1 quart.

1 serving contains:

Cal	Prot	Carb	Fib	Fat	Chol	Sodium
129	3g	29g	0	1g	3mg	46mg

Grape 'n Lemon Frozen Yogurt

Lemon-flavored yogurt lends a delicate flavor to this lemon-grape combination.

1/4 cup water

1 teaspoon unflavored gelatin

1-1/2 cups Concord grape juice

1/3 cup sugar

1/2 cup lowfat milk

1 tablespoon light corn syrup

1 cup lemon lowfat yogurt, stirred

In small saucepan, combine water and gelatin; let stand 1 minute. Cook and stir over low heat until gelatin dissolves; remove from heat. In medium bowl, combine grape juice, sugar, milk, corn syrup and dissolved gelatin. Stir in yogurt. Freeze in ice-cream maker according to manufacturer's directions; or follow refrigerator-freezer instructions on page 4. Makes about 1 quart.

1 serving contains:

Cal	Prot	Carb	Fib	Fat	Chol	Sodium
107	3g	23g	0	1g	2mg	27mg

Watermelon Punch Frozen Yogurt

Do not add water to the frozen fruit punch; the concentrated juices provide a refreshing fruit taste.

1 cup cubed and seeded watermelon

1/3 cup sugar

1 teaspoon unflavored gelatin

1/4 cup water

1 (6-oz.) can frozen red fruit punch concentrate, thawed

1 tablespoon black-raspberry liqueur, optional

3/4 cup plain lowfat yogurt, stirred

In blender or food processor fitted with metal blade, purée watermelon and sugar. In small saucepan, sprinkle gelatin on water; let stand 1 minute. Cook and stir over low heat until gelatin dissolves. Mix with puréed melon. Add fruit punch concentrate and liqueur, if desired. Stir in yogurt. Freeze in ice-cream maker according to manufacturer's directions; or follow refrigerator-freezer instructions on page 4. Makes about 1 quart.

1 serving contains:

Cal	Prot	Carb	Fib	Fat	Chol	Sodium
90	2g	20g	0	0	1mg	18mg

Honeydew Refresher

Keep this recipe in mind when you're looking for a midsummer dessert or snack.

1/4 cup water

1 teaspoon unflavored gelatin

1 (6-oz.) can frozen lemonade concentrate

1-1/2 cups honeydew melon cubes (about 1/2 medium melon)

1/4 cup sugar

1 cup vanilla lowfat yogurt, stirred

In small pan, combine water and gelatin; let stand 1 minute. Cook and stir over low heat until gelatin dissolves; set aside. Partially thaw lemonade concentrate but do not reconstitute. In medium bowl, combine lemonade concentrate and dissolved gelatin. In blender or food processor fitted with metal blade, purée melon with sugar. Add to lemonade mixture. Stir in yogurt. Freeze in ice-cream maker according to manufacturer's directions; or follow refrigerator-freezer instructions on page 4. Makes about 1 quart.

1 serving contains:

Cal	Prot	Carb	Fib	Fat	Chol	Sodium
102	3g	23g	1g	0	1mg	24mg

Honey Gingered Cantaloupe Frozen Yogurt

Freshly grated ginger brings out the best in cantaloupe-orange combination.

2 cups cubed and seeded cantaloupe

1 teaspoon grated fresh ginger

1/2 teaspoon grated orange peel

2 tablespoons honey

1/2 cup sugar

1 teaspoon unflavored gelatin

1/2 cup orange juice

1 cup plain lowfat yogurt

In blender or food processor fitted with metal blade, combine cantaloupe, ginger, orange peel, honey and sugar. Process until puréed. In small saucepan sprinkle gelatin over orange juice; let stand 1 minute. Cook and stir over low heat until gelatin dissolves. Add to puréed fruit mixture. Stir in yogurt. Freeze in ice-cream maker according to manufacturer's directions; or follow refrigerator-freezer instructions on page 4. Makes about 1 quart.

1 serving contains:

Cal	Prot	Carb	Fib	Fat	Chol	Sodium
108	3g	24g	1g	1g	2mg	25mg

Cookies, Candies & Nuts

Oreo® Crumble

Grasshopper Frozen Yogurt

Peanut-butter Cups Frozen Yogurt

Frozen Chocolate Mint Parfait

Peppermint Stick Freeze

Pastel Mint Frozen Yogurt

Café au Lait Frozen Yogurt

Caramel Peanut Butter Frozen Yogurt

Dreamy Peanut Butter Frozen Yogurt

Praline Creme

Yogurt Pralines

Burnt Sugar Frozen Yogurt

Butterscotch Smoothie

Maple Pecan Frozen Yogurt

Crunchy Toffee Bar Favorite

Frozen Butterfinger® Crumble

White Chocolate Macadamia Treat

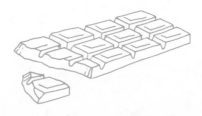

Oreo® Crumble

It takes about 8 double cookies with filling to make enough crumble.

2 teaspoons cornstarch

1/2 cup sugar

1 egg, slightly beaten

1-1/2 cups lowfat milk

1 teaspoon vanilla extract

1 cup plain lowfat yogurt, stirred

8 Oreo® Cookies*, coarsely chopped (1 cup)

*If this recipe will be frozen in a refrigerator freezer, see page 4 or 5 before adding the remaining 1/2 cup chopped cookies.

In medium saucepan, combine cornstarch and sugar. Stir in egg and milk. Cook and stir over moderate heat until mixture simmers and thickens slightly. Cook and stir about 2 minutes longer. Remove from heat; cool. Add vanilla and yogurt to cool egg mixture; then stir in *1/2 cup* chopped cookies. Freeze in ice-cream maker according to manufacturer's directions. When frozen stir in remaining 1/2 cup chopped cookies. Or follow refrigerator-freezer instructions on page 4. Stir in remaining 1/2 cup chopped cookies after final processing or beating. Makes about 1 quart.

1 serving contains:

Cal	Prot	Carb	Fib	Fat	Chol	Sodium
158	4g	26g	0	4g	30mg	111mg

Grasshopper Frozen Yogurt

Enhance your reputation as a hostess by serving this dessert at your next dinner party.

1 cup lowfat milk

1 (1.3-oz.) envelope whipped topping mix

1/4 cup sugar

3 tablespoons green crème de menthe liqueur

2 tablespoons white crème de cacao liqueur

1-1/2 cups plain lowfat yogurt, stirred

6 to 8 chocolate cookies, crushed (about 1/2 cup coarse crumbs)

In medium bowl, gradually add milk to topping mix; stir until well mixed. Add sugar, crème de menthe and crème de cacao. Stir in yogurt. Freeze in ice-cream maker according to manufacturer's directions; or follow refrigerator-freezer instructions on page 4. At serving time, sprinkle about 1 tablespoon crushed chocolate cookies over each serving. Makes about 1 quart.

1 serving contains:

Cal	Prot	Carb	Fib	Fat	Chol	Sodium
184	4g	26g	0	5g	10mg	82mg

Peanut-butter Cups Frozen Yogurt

Peanut-butter cups are available in different sizes. The 2 peanut-butter-cup package weighs slightly under 1 oz. per cup. It takes 16 to 18 miniature cups to make 4 oz.

2 teaspoons cornstarch

1/3 cup sugar

4 oz. milk chocolate

1/4 cup light corn syrup

1-1/4 cups lowfat milk

1/2 teaspoon vanilla extract

1 cup plain lowfat yogurt, stirred

4 oz. peanut-butter cups, chopped

In medium saucepan, combine cornstarch and sugar. Stir in milk chocolate, corn syrup and milk. Cook and stir over medium heat until mixture simmers and chocolate melts. Remove from heat. Stir in vanilla and yogurt; cool. Freeze in ice-cream maker according to manufacturer's directions. When frozen stir in chopped peanut-butter cups. Or follow refrigerator-freezer instructions on page 4 or 5, and stir in chopped peanut butter cups after final processing or beating. Makes about 1 quart.

1 serving contains:

Cal	Prot	Carb	Fib	Fat	Chol	Sodium
245	6g	35g	1g	10g	7mg	84mg

Frozen Chocolate Mint Parfait

Crème de menthe wafers are small rectangles of soft, pale green mint candy sandwiched between two layers of smooth chocolate.

1 cup lowfat milk

1 teaspoon unflavored gelatin

1/2 cup sugar

1-1/2 cups plain lowfat yogurt, stirred

18 pieces (about 3 oz.) chocolate crème de menthe candy wafers (Andes® Daydreams™ by Suchard), finely chopped

3 or 4 drops green food coloring, optional

In 1-quart saucepan, combine milk and gelatin; let stand 1 minute. Add sugar; stir over low heat until gelatin dissolves; cool. Stir in yogurt and finely chopped wafers. Add food coloring, if desired. Freeze in ice-cream maker according to manufacturer's directions; or follow refrigerator-freezer instructions on page 4. Makes about 1 quart.

1 serving contains:

Cal	Prot	Carb	Fib	Fat	Chol	Sodium
148	5g	23g	0	4g	4mg	52mg

Peppermint Stick Freeze

For a festive presentation, sprinkle extra crushed peppermint over each serving.

1 cup lowfat milk

1 teaspoon unflavored gelatin

1/2 cup sugar

1/2 cup crushed peppermint stick candy (about 2-3/4 oz.)*

1-1/2 cups plain lowfat yogurt, stirred

*If this recipe will be frozen in a refrigerator freezer, see page 4 or 5 before adding the remaining half of this ingredient.

In small saucepan, combine milk and gelatin; let stand one minute. Stir over low heat until gelatin dissolves; add sugar. Combine with one-half of the crushed peppermint candy. Cool; stir in yogurt. Freeze in ice-cream maker according to manufacturer's directions. When frozen stir in remaining crushed peppermint. Or follow refrigerator-freezer instructions on page 4. Stir in remaining peppermint after final processing or beating. Makes about 1 quart.

1 serving contains:

Cal	Prot	Carb	Fib	Fat	Chol	Sodium
129	4g	26g	0	1g	4mg	49mg

Pastel Mint Frozen Yogurt

A refreshing, after-dinner dessert.

1 cup lowfat milk

1 (1.3-oz.) envelope Dream Whip® whipped topping mix

1/3 cup sugar

1-1/2 cups plain lowfat yogurt, stirred

3/4 cup (about 4 oz.) pastel after-dinner mints, coarsely chopped*

*If this recipe will be frozen in a refrigerator freezer, see page 4 or 5 before adding this ingredient.

In medium bowl, gradually add milk to whipped topping mix; stir until well mixed. Stir in sugar and yogurt. Add coarsely chopped mints and freeze in ice-cream maker according to manufacturer's directions. Or follow refrigerator-freezer instructions on page 4 and add coarsely chopped mints after final processing or beating. Makes about 1 quart.

1 serving contains:

Cal	Prot	Carb	Fib	Fat	Chol	Sodium
150	3g	29g	0	3g	4mg	79mg

Café au Lait Frozen Yogurt

A mouth-watering mild coffee flavor that tastes like it's loaded with whipping cream.

2/3 cup sugar

2 teaspoons cornstarch

1-1/4 cups lowfat milk

1 tablespoon instant coffee granules

1 egg

1/4 cup miniature or cut-up large marshmallows

1/2 teaspoon vanilla extract

1-1/2 cups plain lowfat yogurt, stirred

In 1-1/2- or 2-quart saucepan, combine sugar and cornstarch. Stir in milk and instant coffee. Cook and stir over medium heat until mixture simmers. In small bowl, beat egg slightly; stir about 1/2 cup hot mixture into beaten egg. Pour egg mixture into pan with remaining hot liquid. Cook and stir over low heat until slightly thickened. Remove from heat; add marshmallows and stir until dissolved. Cool. Stir in vanilla and yogurt. Freeze in ice-cream maker according to manufacturer's directions; or follow refrigerator-freezer instructions on page 4. Makes about 1 quart.

1 serving contains:

Cal	Prot	Carb	Fib	Fat	Chol	Sodium
125	4g	24g	0	2g	30mg	60mg

Caramel Peanut Butter Frozen Yogurt

You can substitute 1 teaspoon vanilla extract and 1 cup plain lowfat yogurt for 1 cup vanilla yogurt.

7 oz. Kraft® caramel squares (about 25 squares)

1-1/2 cups nonfat milk

1/2 cup peanut butter (creamy or chunky)

1 cup lowfat vanilla yogurt, stirred

Remove and discard candy caramel wrappers. In 1-quart saucepan, combine caramels and milk. Cook over very low heat, stirring frequently, about 8 to 10 minutes or until caramels dissolve. Add peanut butter and continue cooking and stirring until mixture is well blended. Remove from heat; cool. Stir in yogurt. Freeze in ice-cream maker according to manufacturer's directions; or follow refrigerator-freezer instructions on page 4. Makes about 1 quart.

1 serving contains:

Cal	Prot	Carb	Fib	Fat	Chol	Sodium
236	8g	28g	1g	11g	3mg	163mg

Dreamy Peanut Butter Frozen Yogurt

Rich tasting, peanut-butter flavor is reminiscent of ice cream made with lots of egg yolks and whipping cream.

1/3 cup chunky peanut butter

2/3 cup brown sugar, lightly packed

1/2 teaspoon vanilla extract

1-1/2 cups lowfat milk

1 (1.3-oz.) envelope Dream Whip® whipped topping mix

1 cup plain lowfat yogurt, stirred

In medium bowl, combine peanut butter, brown sugar and vanilla; set aside. In small bowl, gradually add milk to dry whipped topping mix; stir until well mixed. Gradually stir into peanut butter mixture; then add yogurt. Freeze in ice-cream maker according to manufacturer's directions; or follow refrigerator-freezer instructions on page 4. Makes about 1 quart.

1 serving contains:

Cal	Prot	Carb	Fib	Fat	Chol	Sodium
195	6g	26g	1g	8g	4mg	100mg

Praline Crème

Make your own yogurt pralines (see page 122) or purchase commercially made pralines to use in the recipe.

3/4 cup sugar

1/4 teaspoon baking soda

1/2 cup plain lowfat yogurt, stirred

1 teaspoon vanilla extract

1 tablespoon margarine or butter, optional

2 teaspoons cornstarch

1-1/2 cups low fat milk

1-1/4 cups plain lowfat yogurt, stirred

2 (3-inch) pralines, chopped into 1/2-inch pieces

In 1-1/2- or 2-quart heavy sauce-pan, combine sugar and soda. Add 1/2 cup yogurt and stir until ingredients are well blended. Cook over low heat without stir-ring 5 minutes or until mixture be-gins to boil. Reduce heat to very low and simmer about 10 minutes until foamy mixture no longer in-creases in volume. Remove from heat; stir syrup down. Return to very low heat; simmer 10 to 15 minutes until syrup is a light-cara-mel color. Remove from heat; stir in vanilla and margarine or butter, if desired, until well blended in syrup. Set aside. In small sauce-pan, dissolve cornstarch in milk. Cook and stir over low heat until mixture begins to simmer; then stir or whisk into syrup. Cool syrup; stir in 1-1/4 cups yogurt. Freeze in ice-cream maker accord-ing to manufacturer's directions. When frozen stir in chopped pralines. Or follow refrigerator-freezer instructions on page 4 or 5, and stir in chopped pralines after final processing or beating. Makes about 1 quart.

1 serving contains:

Cal	Prot	Carb	Fib	Fat	Chol	Sodium
173	5g	31g	0	4g	5mg	96mg

Yogurt Pralines

If you don't have complete confidence in your candy thermometer's accuracy, also use the cold-water, soft-ball test.

1 cup sugar

1/4 teaspoon baking soda

1/2 cup plain lowfat yogurt, stirred

1/2 teaspoon vanilla extract

1 tablespoon margarine or butter

1 cup chopped pecans

In 1-1/2- or 2-quart heavy saucepan, thoroughly combine sugar and soda. Add yogurt and stir until ingredients are well blended. Cook over low heat without stirring about 5 minutes or until mixture begins to boil. Reduce heat to very low and simmer about 10 minutes until foamy mixture no longer increases in volume. Remove from heat; stir syrup down. Return to very low heat and attach a candy thermometer to side of saucepan, making sure bulb does not touch bottom of pan. Simmer 10 to 12 minutes, without stirring, until syrup reaches 238F (115C) on candy thermometer. It should form a soft ball in cold water (syrup mounds when dropped in cold water and ball flattens when held out of water on a finger tip). Remove from heat; stir in vanilla and margarine or butter until well incorporated in syrup. Add pecans; stir until well distributed. Spoon onto waxed paper making 3-inch patties. Cool. Makes about 9 (3-inch) pralines.

1 praline contains:

Cal	Prot	Carb	Fib	Fat	Chol	Sodium
193	2g	25g	1g	10g	1mg	47mg

Burnt Sugar Frozen Yogurt

Although the popular name for this process is Burnt Sugar, *it should be heated to a beautiful golden color, not dark brown.*

3/4 cup sugar

1 (12-oz.) can evaporated lowfat milk

1 egg, slightly beaten

1 teaspoon vanilla extract

1-1/2 cups plain lowfat yogurt, stirred

In heavy 10-inch skillet, cook sugar over moderate heat until it becomes a caramel-colored liquid. Remove from heat. Gradually stir in milk. Return to low heat; stir until smooth. Stir small amount of milk mixture into beaten egg; return to skillet. Cook and stir over low heat 3 to 4 minutes until mixture thickens and coats a metal spoon. Remove from heat; cool. Stir in vanilla and yogurt. Freeze in ice-cream maker according to manufacturer's directions; or follow refrigerator-freezer instructions on page 4. Makes about 1 quart.

1 serving contains:

Cal	Prot	Carb	Fib	Fat	Chol	Sodium
142	6g	27g	0	1g	30mg	88mg

Butterscotch Smoothie

So rich and smooth that your guests will think it's loaded with whipping cream.

2/3 cup dark brown sugar, lightly packed

2 teaspoons cornstarch

1/4 cup dark corn syrup

1 (12-oz.) can lowfat evaporated milk

1 egg, slightly beaten

1/2 teaspoon vanilla extract

1 cup plain lowfat yogurt, stirred

1/4 cup chopped toasted pecans, optional*

*If this recipe will be frozen in a refrigerator freezer, please see page 4 or 5 before adding this ingredient.

In medium saucepan, combine brown sugar and cornstarch. Stir in corn syrup, milk and beaten egg. Cook and stir over *medium-low* heat until mixture simmers; cook and stir 2 minutes longer. Remove from heat; cool. Stir in vanilla, yogurt and pecans, if desired. Freeze in ice-cream maker according to manufacturer's directions; or follow refrigerator-freezer instructions on page 4. Stir in pecans if desired, after final processing or beating. Makes about 1 quart.

1 serving contains:

Cal	Prot	Carb	Fib	Fat	Chol	Sodium
161	5g	33g	0	1g	29mg	92mg

Maple Pecan Frozen Yogurt

Stores well in refrigerator-freezer without losing its smooth, rich texture.

1/2 cup chopped pecans*

3/4 cup lowfat milk

1 egg, slightly beaten

1 cup maple-flavored syrup

1/2 teaspoon vanilla extract

1 cup plain lowfat yogurt, stirred

*If this recipe will be frozen in a refrigerator freezer, please see page 4 or 5 before adding this ingredient.

Place pecans in pie pan. Heat in 350F (177C) oven about 10 minutes or until lightly toasted; set aside to cool. In medium saucepan, combine milk, beaten egg and maple-flavored syrup. Cook and stir over medium-low heat until slightly thickened. Remove from heat; cool. Add vanilla, toasted pecans and yogurt. Freeze in ice-cream maker according to manufacturer's directions; or follow refrigerator-freezer instructions on page 4. Makes about 1 quart.

1 serving contains:

Cal	Prot	Carb	Fib	Fat	Chol	Sodium
186	4g	30g	0	6g	29mg	46mg

Crunchy Toffee Bar Favorite

For a crunchier texture and more pronounced toffee flavor, make this frozen yogurt with three double candy bars.

1 (12-oz.) can evaporated lowfat milk

1 teaspoon unflavored gelatin

1/3 cup brown sugar

2 or 3 double Heath® bars (about 2-1/4 to 3-1/2 ounces)

1 cup plain lowfat yogurt, stirred

In a small saucepan, combine milk and gelatin; let stand one minute. Stir over low heat until gelatin dissolves. Add sugar; cool. Cut candy bars into quarters; coarsely crush in blender or food processor fitted with metal blade. Stir crushed candy and yogurt into milk mixture. Freeze in ice-cream maker according to manufacturer's directions; or follow refrigerator-freezer instructions on page 4. Makes about 1 quart.

1 serving contains:

Cal	Prot	Carb	Fib	Fat	Chol	Sodium
144	6g	18g	0	5g	3mg	96mg

Frozen Butterfinger® Crumble

It's light and fluffy with tiny pieces of Butterfinger® bars.

1 cup lowfat milk

1 (1.3-oz.) envelope Dream Whip® whipped topping mix

1/3 cup sugar

2 regular-size Butterfinger® bars (about 4 ounces)

1-1/2 cups plain lowfat yogurt, stirred

1/2 teaspoon vanilla extract

In medium bowl, gradually add milk to topping mix; stir until well mixed. Add sugar. Quarter candy bars; coarsely crush in blender or food processor fitted with metal blade. Stir crushed candy, yogurt and vanilla into milk mixture. Freeze in ice-cream maker according to manufacturer's directions; or follow refrigerator-freezer instructions on page 4. Makes about 1 quart.

1 serving contains:

Cal	Prot	Carb	Fib	Fat	Chol	Sodium
132	4g	20g	0	4g	4mg	64mg

White Chocolate Macadamia Treat

Or, substitute a white chocolate with almonds candy bar and leave out the macadamias.

1 cup lowfat milk

1/4 cup sugar

2 tablespoons light corn syrup

1 (8-oz.) carton egg substitute (Egg Beaters®), thawed

4 oz. white baking bar or white chocolate candy bar, finely chopped

1/4 cup macadamia nuts, coarsely chopped*

1/2 teaspoon vanilla extract

1 cup plain lowfat yogurt, stirred

*If this recipe will be frozen in a refrigerator freezer, please see page 4 or 5 before adding this ingredient.

In 2-quart saucepan, combine milk, sugar, corn syrup and egg substitute. Stir until well blended. Cook and stir over moderate heat until mixture is very thick. Remove from heat; immediately stir in chopped white chocolate. Add macadamia nuts and vanilla; cool. Stir in yogurt. Freeze in ice-cream maker according to manufacturer's directions; or follow refrigerator-freezer instructions on page 4. Makes about 1 quart.

1 serving contains:

Cal	Prot	Carb	Fib	Fat	Chol	Sodium
224	7g	23g	0	12g	3mg	110mg

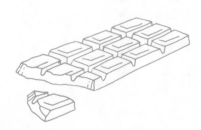

Pickups

Fresh Plum Yogurt Pickups

Purple Cow Pops

Walk-Away Melba Cups

Vineyard Citrus Glaciers

Watermelon Berry Yogurt Pops

Frozen Yogurt S'Mores Cups

Peanut Butter 'n Jelly Pops

Sunrise Yogurt Cups

Fresh Plum Yogurt Pickups

Popular fresh-fruit flavors team up for a nutritious change-of-pace snack.

1/2 cup orange juice

1 teaspoon unflavored gelatin

4 fresh plums, seeded and quartered

3 tablespoons sugar

2 tablespoons honey

1 cup lowfat vanilla yogurt, stirred

In small saucepan, combine orange juice and gelatin; let stand 1 minute. Cook and stir over low heat until gelatin dissolves. Remove from heat; set aside. In blender or food processor fitted with metal blade, combine plums, sugar and honey. Process until plums are finely chopped. In a bowl, combine plum mixture, dissolved gelatin and yogurt. Spoon into 8 (3-oz.) paper cups or 12 (2-oz.) popsicle molds. Place in refrigerator-freezer until partially frozen. Insert stick in each cup or mold. Freeze until firm. To serve, peel off paper cups or dip plastic mold in lukewarm water very briefly and remove frozen-yogurt pickups from mold. Makes 8 (3-oz.) or 12 (2-oz.) servings.

1 serving contains:

Cal	Prot	Carb	Fib	Fat	Chol	Sodium
87	3g	19g	1g	1g	1mg	21mg

Purple Cow Pops

So quick, easy, and delicious.

3/4 cup Concord grape juice

1/4 cup light corn syrup

3/4 cup plain lowfat yogurt, stirred

In medium bowl, combine grape juice and corn syrup. Stir in yogurt. Pour into 6 or 8 plastic popsicle molds or paper cups (2 or 3 oz.). Place in refrigerator-freezer until partially frozen. Insert stick in each cup or mold. Freeze until firm. To serve, peel off paper cups or dip plastic mold in lukewarm water very briefly and remove frozen-yogurt pops from mold. Makes 6 (3-oz.) or 8 (2-oz.) pops.

1 pop contains:

Cal	Prot	Carb	Fib	Fat	Chol	Sodium
75	2g	17g	0	0	2mg	27mg

Walk-Away Melba Cups

Handy to have on hand in the freezer for children of all ages.

1 cup miniature marshmallows

1/4 cup lowfat milk

1 ripe peach, peeled and quartered

1/4 cup fresh or frozen unsweetened raspberries or strawberries

1 cup lowfat peach yogurt, stirred

In small saucepan, melt marshmallows in milk over low heat; set aside to cool. In blender or food processor fitted with metal blade, finely chop peach and berries. Add to cool marshmallow mixture and stir in yogurt. Spoon into 6 (3-oz.) paper cups or 8 (2-oz.) plastic popsicle molds. Place in refrigerator-freezer until partially frozen. Insert stick in each cup or mold. Freeze until firm. To serve, peel off paper cups or dip plastic mold in lukewarm water very briefly and remove frozen yogurt from mold. Makes 6 (3-oz.) or 8 (2-oz.) servings.

1 serving contains:

Cal	Prot	Carb	Fib	Fat	Chol	Sodium
81	2g	18g	1g	1g	2mg	34mg

Vineyard Citrus Glaciers

Be sure to use fresh, dark-purple, Concord grapes; other varieties will yield an entirely different product.

1 cup Concord grapes

1/3 cup sugar

2 tablespoons honey

1/2 cup orange juice

1 cup plain lowfat yogurt, stirred

In blender or food processor fitted with metal blade, purée grapes with sugar. Strain; discard seeds and skin. In medium bowl, combine purée with honey and orange juice; stir in yogurt. Pour into 6 (3-oz.) paper cups or 8 (2-oz.) plastic popsicle molds. Place in refrigerator-freezer until partially frozen. Insert stick in each cup or mold. Freeze until firm. To serve, peel off paper cups or dip plastic mold in luke-warm water very briefly and remove frozen yogurt from mold. Makes 6 (3-oz.) or 8 (2-oz.) servings.

1 serving contains:

Cal	Prot	Carb	Fib	Fat	Chol	Sodium
107	2g	24g	0	1g	2mg	28mg

Watermelon Berry Yogurt Pops

A sophisticated combination of flavors that appeals to adults as well as children.

1/2 cup fresh or frozen unsweetened raspberries

2 cups watermelon cubes, seeded

1/2 cup sugar

1/8 teaspoon almond extract

1 cup plain lowfat or nonfat yogurt, stirred

In blender or food processor fitted with metal blade, purée raspberries. Strain; discard seeds. Purée watermelon with sugar. In medium bowl, combine strained raspberries, puréed watermelon, almond extract and yogurt. Pour into 9 (3-oz.) paper cups. Place in refrigerator-freezer. When partially frozen, or after about 1 hour, insert wooden stick in center of each pop. Freeze until firm. To serve, remove paper cups. Makes 9 pops.

1 pop contains:

Cal	Prot	Carb	Fib	Fat	Chol	Sodium
73	2g	16g	1g	1g	2mg	19mg

Frozen Yogurt S'Mores Cups

A new variation of traditional flavors associated with snacks around the campfire.

1/2 cup crushed graham crackers (about 6 squares)

1 tablespoon melted margarine or butter

1 cup chocolate *frozen* yogurt, page 16, slightly softened

1/4 cup marshmallow cream, stirred

1/2 teaspoon lukewarm water

In small bowl, combine graham-cracker crumbs and margarine or butter. Line 4 custard cups with paper baking liners. Press about *half* of crumb mixture on bottom of liners; chill. Working quickly, lightly press *half* of frozen chocolate yogurt over chilled graham-cracker mixture. Stir marshmallow cream with lukewarm water until smooth; spoon over yogurt in each cup. Then top with remaining frozen yogurt. Sprinkle with remaining crumb mixture. Freeze in refrigerator-freezer at least 2 hours or until firm. Makes 4.

1 serving contains:

Cal	Prot	Carb	Fib	Fat	Chol	Sodium
185	3g	34g	1g	5g	7mg	161mg

Peanut Butter 'n Jelly Pops

Classic all-American combination that's a favorite with all ages.

3/4 cup lowfat milk

1 teaspoon cornstarch

2 tablespoons peanut butter

1/3 cup brown sugar, lightly packed

1/2 teaspoon vanilla extract

3/4 cup plain lowfat yogurt, stirred

6 or 7 teaspoons grape jelly or strawberry jam

In medium saucepan, combine milk and cornstarch. Cook and stir over moderate heat until mixture simmers; stir in peanut butter and brown sugar. Remove from heat; cool. Stir in vanilla and yogurt. Spoon into 6 or 7 (2 or 3 oz.) frozen-pop molds or paper cups. Partially freeze in refrigerator-freezer. Spoon about 1 teaspoon jelly or jam on top of each cup or mold; swirl with table knife. Insert a popsicle stick in each. Return to refrigerator-freezer, freeze until firm. To serve, peel off paper cups or dip plastic mold in lukewarm water very briefly and remove frozen yogurt from mold. Makes 6 or 7 frozen pops.

1 pop contains:

Cal	Prot	Carb	Fib	Fat	Chol	Sodium
126	4g	21g	0	4g	3mg	64mg

Sunrise Yogurt Cups

When frozen, carefully peel off paper cups or quickly dip plastic molds into lukewarm water and pull frozen mixture out of individual mold.

1 (3-oz.) package orange-flavored gelatin

1 cup boiling water

1 cup orange juice

1 banana, peeled and mashed

1 cup plain lowfat yogurt, stirred

In small bowl, dissolve gelatin in boiling water. Stir in orange juice, banana and yogurt. Spoon into 15 (2-oz.) paper cups or 10 (3-oz.) popsicle molds. Place in refrigerator-freezer until partially frozen. Insert stick in each cup or mold. Freeze until firm. To serve, peel off paper cups or dip plastic mold in lukewarm water very briefly and remove frozen yogurt from mold. Makes 10 (3-oz.) or 15 (2-oz.) cups.

1 serving contains:

Cal	Prot	Carb	Fib	Fat	Chol	Sodium
45	2g	9g	0	0	2mg	22mg

Molded Deserts

Sweet Pizza Yogurt Sundae

Frozen Raspberry Trifle

Crunchy Yogurt Bars

Frozen Chocolate Cheese Pie

Toasted Angel Loaf Shortcake

Frozen Apricot Gingersnap Cheesecake

Chocolate Rim Sandwiches

Sweet Pizza Yogurt Sundae

Mix and match with your favorite toppings; garnish with maraschino cherry halves or sliced strawberries, if desired.

1 (20-oz.) package refrigerated sugar-cookie dough

1 quart vanilla or chocolate *frozen* yogurt, page 10 or 16

1/3 cup chocolate or fudge sauce, or Velvet Fudge Sauce, page 150

1/4 cup raspberry or strawberry sauce, or Ruby Red Sauce, page 149

6 tablespoons non-dairy whipped topping, or Yogurt Whipped Topping, page 148

1/4 cup chopped pecans or pistachios

Preheat oven to 350F (177C). Roll out refrigerated cookie dough between 2 sheets of waxed paper to 12-1/2 inches round. Remove top layer of waxed paper. Lift up bottom paper holding rolled-out dough. Invert; place dough on 12-inch pizza pan. Remove waxed paper. Press dough lightly along bottom and sides of pan. Prick every 2 inches with fork. Bake in preheated oven about 15 minutes or until golden brown; cool. Cover cooled dough unevenly with *frozen* yogurt. With teaspoon, make small pools of chocolate or fudge sauce every 2 inches over frozen yogurt. Make pools of raspberry sauce between chocolate sauce. Top with small mounds of whipped topping. Sprinkle with nuts. Serve immediately or store in refrigerator-freezer. Cut into 8 wedges.

1 serving contains:

Cal	Prot	Carb	Fib	Fat	Chol	Sodium
599	10g	89g	1g	24g	73mg	492mg

Frozen Raspberry Trifle

An easy-to-make trifle featuring bakery cake and two kinds of frozen yogurt.

1/2 cup seedless raspberry jam

1 tablespoon Chambord black-raspberry liqueur

1 (l-lb.) loaf pound cake, cut into 15 crosswise slices

1 pint vanilla *frozen* yogurt, slightly softened, page 10

1 pint raspberry *frozen* yogurt, slightly softened, page 34

1 egg white

1/3 cup nonfat dry milk

1/3 cup water

2 tablespoons sugar

Line 9 x 5-inch loaf pan with foil or waxed paper. In small bowl, combine jam and liqueur. Set aside about 1 tablespoon jam mixture for garnish. Lightly coat one side of each slice of cake with remaining jam mixture. Line bottom and sides of loaf pan with 9 slices of cake, placing uncoated side of cake against outside and bottom of pan. Carefully spread *frozen* vanilla yogurt over cake in bottom of pan. Place 3 slices of cake, jam-side down, on *frozen* vanilla yogurt. Carefully spread *frozen* raspberry yogurt over cake. Top with remaining slices of cake, jam-side down. If any pieces of cake are higher than the pan, trim even with top. Freeze until firm. Unmold and remove foil or waxed paper. Beat egg white, nonfat dry milk and water until stiff but not dry. Beat in sugar. Frost top and sides of frozen loaf. Drizzle reserved 1 tablespoon jam over top. Serve immediately or refreeze. Cut crosswise into 8 or 9 slices.

1 serving contains:

Cal	Prot	Carb	Fib	Fat	Chol	Sodium
441	10g	79g	2g	12g	142mg	298mg

Crunchy Yogurt Bars

To break up pieces of cereal, put them in a heavy plastic bag, then coarsely crush them with a rolling pin.

1/2 cup coarsely chopped peanuts

2 cups coarsely crushed Cracklin' Oat Bran® cereal

2 tablespoons honey

3 tablespoons melted margarine or butter

1 quart vanilla, chocolate or orange *frozen* yogurt, page 10, 16 or 68

In large bowl, combine peanuts, cereal and honey. Add margarine or butter; toss until evenly coated. Line 8-inch-square baking pan with waxed paper. Spread *half* of cereal mixture on bottom of pan. Spread *frozen* yogurt over cereal; top with remaining cereal mixture. Press cereal lightly into *frozen* yogurt. Cover with plastic wrap or foil; freeze in refrigerator-freezer at least 2 hours or until yogurt is firm. Cut into 12 bars. Place each bar in a small plastic bag. Freeze again if too soft. Let each person pick up and eat individual serving in plastic bag. Makes 12 bars.

1 serving contains:

Cal	Prot	Carb	Fib	Fat	Chol	Sodium
209	7g	30g	2g	8g	20mg	161mg

Frozen Chocolate Cheese Pie

A double chocolate dessert designed just for chocoholics.

1 cup crushed chocolate cookies (18 to 20)

2 tablespoons melted margarine or butter

1 cup cottage cheese

3/4 cup sugar

1/2 cup unsweetened cocoa powder

1/2 teaspoon vanilla extract

1 cup plain lowfat yogurt

2 egg whites

In small bowl, combine crushed cookies and margarine or butter. Press on bottom and sides of 9-inch pie pan; chill. In blender or food processor fitted with metal blade, combine cottage cheese, sugar, unsweetened cocoa powder, vanilla and yogurt. Process until cottage cheese is smooth. In medium bowl, beat egg whites until stiff but not dry. Gradually fold in smooth cottage-cheese mixture. Spoon into crumb-lined pie pan. Cover with plastic wrap or foil and freeze in refrigerator-freezer for 4 hours or until firm. Cut into 6 or 8 wedges.

1 wedge contains:

Cal	Prot	Carb	Fib	Fat	Chol	Sodium
434	12g	65g	3g	16g	34mg	353mg

Toasted Angel Loaf Shortcake

Even a novice cook can impress guests with this memorable dessert.

1 angel food loaf cake (about 7 x 3 inches)

3 cups fresh or frozen unsweetened strawberries

1/4 cup sugar

1 quart vanilla or strawberry *frozen* yogurt, page 10 or 28

8 tablespoons non-dairy whipped topping, or Yogurt Whipped Topping, page 148

Cut cake crosswise into 8 slices. Lightly toast both sides; cool. Cap and slice berries; stir in sugar. Spoon *frozen* yogurt over slices of cake; then top with sliced berries. Garnish with whipped topping. Makes 8 servings.

1 serving contains:

Cal	Prot	Carb	Fib	Fat	Chol	Sodium
326	10g	69g	2g	2g	31mg	363mg

Frozen Apricot Gingersnap Cheesecake

Avoid last-minute preparation with this special make-ahead dessert.

1-1/2 cups crushed gingersnaps (about 24 cookies)

1/4 cup melted margarine or butter

1 cup lowfat milk

1 teaspoon unflavored gelatin

1 (8-oz.) package Neufchatel cheese, cubed

3/4 cup sugar

1/4 teaspoon almond extract

3/4 cup dried apricots, coarsely chopped

1 cup plain lowfat yogurt, stirred

In small bowl, combine crushed cookies and margarine or butter. Press on bottom and about 2 inches up sides of 8-inch spring-form pan; refrigerate. In small saucepan, combine milk and gelatin; let stand 1 minute. Cook and stir over low heat until gelatin dissolves; remove from heat. In blender or food processor fitted with metal blade, combine cheese, sugar, almond extract and apricots. Process until well blended. Add dissolved gelatin; process very briefly. Stir into yogurt. Spoon into cookie-lined pan. Freeze in refrigerator-freezer until firm (about 2 hours). Makes 1 (8-inch) cheesecake.

1 serving contains:

Cal	Prot	Carb	Fib	Fat	Chol	Sodium
430	9g	53g	2g	21g	35mg	362mg

Chocolate Rim Sandwiches

Pick your favorite homemade or commercial cookie. We enjoy oatmeal, sugar or chocolate-chip cookies in this recipe.

1 pint vanilla or chocolate *frozen* yogurt, slightly softened, page 10 or 16

12 large round cookies (2-1/2 to 2-3/4 inch diameter)

4 oz. semi-sweet or milk chocolate

1-1/2 teaspoons vegetable shortening

Using a medium ice-cream scoop, place a scoop of *frozen* yogurt on the flat side of each of 6 cookies. Top with another cookie, flat side down. Press top cookie down gently until *frozen* yogurt extends to edges of cookies. Smooth edges of yogurt with metal spatula so it is flush with edges of cookies. Freeze at least 2 hours or until firm. Melt chocolate with shortening; cool to room temperature but not until mixture is solid. Remove yogurt sandwiches, one at a time. Quickly roll edges in chocolate. Serve immediately or return to freezer. Makes 6 sandwiches.

1 serving contains:

Cal	Prot	Carb	Fib	Fat	Chol	Sodium
323	6g	46g	1g	15g	35mg	193mg

Sauces & Toppings

Yogurt Whipped Topping

Ruby Red Sauce

Velvet Fudge Sauce

Gingered Suzette Sauce

Root Beer Sauce

Amber Apricot Sauce

Bits & Pieces

Yogurt Whipped Topping

Use this topping within 24 hours after it's made. Or it can be frozen, then thawed, stirred and served.

2-1/2 tablespoons nonfat dry milk

2 tablespoons nonfat milk

1 egg white

2 tablespoons light corn syrup

1/2 cup vanilla lowfat yogurt

In custard or measuring cup, combine dry and liquid milk. Stir until dry milk dissolves; set aside in refrigerator. In small mixer bowl, beat egg white with electric mixer on medium-high speed until foamy. Add corn syrup and chilled milk mixture; continue beating until mixture is glossy and soft peaks form. Fold in yogurt. Cover and refrigerate until used or freeze if it will be used more than 24 hours after it is made. Makes about 1-1/2 cups.

1 tablespoon contains:

Cal	Prot	Carb	Fib	Fat	Chol	Sodium
12	1g	2g	0	0	0	8mg

Ruby Red Sauce

Quick and easy to make, it's a handy topping for yogurt sundaes and parfaits.

2 cups fresh or frozen unsweetened raspberries

1/3 cup currant jelly

1 tablespoon margarine or butter

1/8 teaspoon almond extract

In blender or food processor fitted with metal blade, purée berries. Strain; discard seeds. In small saucepan, combine strained berries, currant jelly and margarine or butter. Stir over low heat until jelly and margarine dissolve. Stir in almond extract; cool to room temperature. Cover and refrigerate until used. Makes 1 cup.

1 tablespoon contains:

Cal	Prot	Carb	Fib	Fat	Chol	Sodium
30	0	6g	1g	1g	0	10mg

Velvet Fudge Sauce

This recipe also makes a great peanut-butter-fudge sauce. Merely stir in 1/4 cup peanut butter after adding the vanilla extract.

2 tablespoons unsweetened cocoa powder

1 cup sugar

1/3 cup nonfat milk

1/8 teaspoon salt

1 tablespoon margarine or butter

1/2 teaspoon vanilla extract

In small saucepan, combine cocoa powder and sugar. Stir until well blended. Add milk and salt; stir until mixture is liquid. Cook over medium-low heat, stirring occasionally, until mixture simmers. Reduce heat; stir in margarine or butter. Simmer about 2 or 3 minutes longer. Remove from heat; stir in vanilla. Cool to room temperature; then cover and refrigerate until used. Makes about 1 cup.

1 tablespoon contains:

Cal	Prot	Carb	Fib	Fat	Chol	Sodium
58	0	13g	0	1g	0	28mg

Gingered Suzette Sauce

Excellent on toasted pound cake, with or without frozen yogurt.

1-1/2 cups orange juice

2 tablespoons sugar

1 teaspoon unflavored gelatin

8 to 10 (1/8-inch-thick) crosswise slices fresh ginger, peeled

In small saucepan, combine orange juice, sugar and gelatin; let stand 1 minute. Add ginger slices; cook and stir over medium-low heat until mixture begins to simmer. Remove from heat; cover and let stand about 10 minutes. Remove and discard ginger slices; cool to room temperature. Cover and refrigerate several hours; then stir before serving. Makes about 1-1/4 cups.

1 tablespoon contains:

Cal	Prot	Carb	Fib	Fat	Chol	Sodium
15	1g	3g	0	0	0	1mg

Root Beer Sauce

An ideal companion for vanilla frozen yogurt.

1 (12-oz.) can root beer

2 teaspoons sugar

1 tablespoon cornstarch

In small saucepan, combine root beer, sugar and cornstarch. Stir until cornstarch is dissolved. Cook and stir over medium-low heat until mixture begins to simmer. Simmer and stir 3 or 4 minutes longer or until thickened slightly. Remove from heat; cool to room temperature. Cover and refrigerate until used. Makes about 1 cup.

1 tablespoon contains:

Cal	Prot	Carb	Fib	Fat	Chol	Sodium
13	0	3g	0	0	0	3mg

Amber Apricot Sauce

Great served over pineapple, banana or other tropical fruit-flavored frozen yogurts.

1 tablespoon cornstarch

2 tablespoons sugar

1 cup apricot nectar

1/4 cup light corn syrup

1 teaspoon lemon juice

In small saucepan, combine cornstarch and sugar. Stir in apricot nectar and corn syrup. Cook and stir over moderate heat until translucent and slightly thickened. Remove from heat. Add lemon juice; cool. Makes about 1-1/4 cups sauce.

1 tablespoon contains:

Cal	Prot	Carb	Fib	Fat	Chol	Sodium
25	0	6g	0	0	0	2mg

Bits & Pieces

Favorite dry toppings to sprinkle over frozen yogurt.

Chopped fresh fruit

Chopped dry fruit

Chopped nuts

Granola and Muesli

Crunchy cereal (crushed)

Oreo® cookies (chopped)

Coconut

M & M's® (chopped)

Chocolate Peanut Butter Cups (chopped) (Reese's®)

Sprinkles (chocolate and multicolored)

Butterfinger® bar (chopped)

Peanut butter chips

Mini chocolate chips

Nonpareils (chopped)

Index